UNDER AN ALGARROBO TREE

Under an Algarrobo Tree

David Leake

A memoir

LOXWOOD PRESS

ISBN 978-1-908113-02-3

First published 2012
Reprinted May 2012, June 2012
Loxwood Press, 50 Loxwood Avenue, Worthing, West Sussex
BN14 7RA
Tel: 01903 232208

Cover photograph: Ossian Lindholm

Printed by Copyzone, Bishop's Stortford

My father Alfred as a boy (in bath chair) with sister Olive and brother Clem

Contents

CONTENTS

Acknowledgements

My wife Rachel, our three children Andrew, Philip and Judith, their spouses María, Victoria and Ken, and our grandchildren Tomás Francesco, María Cecilia, Carolina Sofía, Georgina Maia and Sebastian Alexander have all over the years, and at different stages and places, contributed to the enrichment of an already varied life. My deepest thanks to them all.

Rachel's sensitivity, love, patience and willingness to face different climates, languages and cultures, to bring up a family in often uncertain and unfamiliar circumstances, have made it possible for this story to be told.

My thanks to my extended family, the Toba and Wichi people, without whom there would be no story to tell; also the dispersed Anglicans and many other friends in Buenos Aires and beyond. They have all added colour, joy, amusement and sadness to the wonderful mosaic of a privileged and colourful life.

With regard to the written story, my very special gratitude to Robert Lunt for his encouragement and editorial assistance in shaping my manuscript and creating an index. My thanks also to Bishop Patrick Harris and Bishop Graham James who have suggested the story is worth telling. Robert Lunt put me in touch with Donald Banks, my publisher, to whom I owe a debt of gratitude for maintaining the pressure on me to keep going and for making possible the finished book.

A final thanks to the hundreds of people not mentioned whose lives have touched mine and whose contribution and example have left an indelible mark of eternal value. As someone suggested, their contribution will be recorded by a photocopy sent to heaven.

Preface

THIS is a story of a privileged and rich life; an upbringing that brought with it varied opportunities.

I owe much to my parents who, following the well-known Norfolk dictum of *"du different"*, did just that.

In retirement in the village of East Runton, I reflect on the life style they fully embraced in the forests of northern Argentina amongst the Toba and Wichi (Mataco) people, worlds away from the parochial village life of their fathers, one a fisherman and the other a carpenter.

My father reduced the complex Toba language to writing, produced the first basic Grammar of the language and some selected translations from the Bible; he also learnt Wichi and Spanish.

My mother spoke basic Toba, and made herself understood, as my father described it, by "signs and wonders".

My parents adopted the policy of fully integrating with the Toba people, and had their wedding service and celebration within the Toba community, and my birth and that of my first sister Cristina were in an adobe brick house in the village in the shade of the algarrobo trees.

My first playmates were the Toba children, my first language and first culture were also Toba, and I was cared for by a Toba "nanny.

Those seeking a learned and deep anthropological treatise on the Indians may be disappointed with my story because that is not its purpose; it is simply a story of special circumstances that provided me with experiences and opportunities which I have endeavoured to build on and hopefully used in the service of God. *David Leake*

Foreword

Bishop Patrick Harris

THIS book is different! Travelogue books, television series and accounts of people's visits to the more unreachable parts of the world abound. But this is the fascinating story of someone who did not just visit the Toba and Wichi Indians of Northern Argentina, but who was born, lived and worked amongst them. They live in a remote and inhospitable part of the Gran Chaco, which means 'Hunting Land' and has been called 'The Green Hell'! The story starts in 1927 when David Leake's father went out to this area and concludes over eighty years later, with David's son Andrew currently working as a consultant in the area of land rights and conservation.

The book is full of amusing, vivid and poignant stories, that illustrate the dramatic and historic developments that were taking place during these years in Argentina, including 'The Falklands War'. Understanding the very different cultures and speaking fluently the two Indian languages as well as Spanish gave him the ability to act as a unique mediator and interpreter in these revolutionary times. Bishop David did not just live through them, but he was a significant influence as he identified with these marginalised peoples and stood with them during a period of momentous change.

Around this time, Argentina celebrates its discovery by Spain 500 years ago and its liberation and foundation as a Republic 200 years ago. In this book, we read about the forgotten original inhabitants of this land, who lived here before these events took place but who continue their vibrant way of life to this day. Their story is almost unknown, but this remarkable part of Argentine history needed to be told.

Although David Leake's final ministry was as Bishop in Buenos Aires—1,000 miles and 'light years' away from his earlier experience in the Chaco—he fulfilled a valued and respected role as leader, mediator and conciliator. He was able to do this because he had developed these gifts by learning to sit alongside his Indian brothers and sisters.

Above all, Bishop David with his wife Rachel, by their example, demonstrate how God does lead and guide, if we are ready to be open and listen to him. And then the adventure begins. What an adventure it has been for them—and can be for us.

Alfred and his mother: the Mataco called him "Pites", Tall Man

1

From the North Sea to the Pilcomayo River

THE cliffs at East Runton in Norfolk overlooking the North Sea would seem to have nothing in common with the banks of the River Pilcomayo looking out from Argentina to Paraguay. Yet a gravestone tucked away in West Runton churchyard marks the resting place of a couple born and brought up in the neighbouring community, but whose life and work is better remembered in the distant tribal villages of northern Argentina.

Strange names adorn that stone—*Pites, Locaina,* tribal names given to Alfred and Dorothy Leake who in the years between two world wars left Norfolk to give their lives to two of Argentina's tribal groups. *Pites* is Mataco for Tall Man and *Locaina* means Tall Woman in Toba. Their bearers have now "left the earth", as the tribes say, but their names live on in the culture and lore of the people.

William Alfred Leake, my father, was born in 1902 of fishing stock, his own father and grandfather both having crab boats off the East Runton beach. His education at the village school was interrupted by two years' illness with TB of the stomach. After those truncated schooldays he obtained his first job in Allen's garage in Cromer and later joined the uniformed movement of the Anglican Church known as the Church Army. His shyness and reserve meant his vocation was directed towards the area of social action and the care of young offenders rather than preaching.

Alfred in Church Army uniform

After a few years Alfred ventured to consider missionary work in South America, so one dark, cold, rainy night he went to a meeting in Liverpool. There were not many present, the speaker was boring and long-winded, and the chairman had to pull his coat-tails to bring his talk to a close! Yet from so inauspicious an occasion came Alfred's calling to South America.

Dorothy Violet Frostick was also born and brought up in East Runton and attended the village school on the Lower Common. Her father was a carpenter and the family lived in the High Street. After school, she was apprenticed at Rust's in Cromer and worked as a dressmaker "specialising in fur renovations". Her home was next door to Weight's Garage. The mechanics also undertook bicycle repairs and would tease Dorothy that "there were no need for two belles on a bike!" So she must have been regarded as a good looker! Her early experience in dressmaking and Alfred's in car mechanics were to serve them well in their later years in the isolated north of Argentina.

My mother Dorothy Frostick

Steam and mules

Alfred sailed in 1926 from Tilbury on the steamship *Gelria* and after a stormy crossing arrived in the Argentine capital,

The 'Gelria' on which Alfred sailed to Buenos Aires

Buenos Aires, 30 days later. From there he took the train from the famous Retiro station on a four-day journey to the end of the line. The landlocked frontier town of Embarcación in the northern province of Salta was another world from his beloved North Norfolk coast, but for the shy, reserved young man with an abbreviated basic education it was a dream come true as he travelled the final 40 kilometres through the forest to Misión Chaqueña for his first encounter with the Mataco Indians he had heard about in that meeting in Liverpool. He joined the team of experienced missionaries led by Richard Hunt, a team which included Henry Grubb who many years later would marry Alfred's sister Olive.

Alfred's potential must have been evident to Hunt since he soon selected him to accompany fellow-missionary Colin Smith and some Mataco evangelists on a tour of exploration to the banks of the River Pilcomayo. They planned to visit other groups of Indians living along that frontier with the then Republic of Bolivia.

So while Dorothy cycled each day from East Runton to work in Cromer, Alfred and his companions were crossing the dry forests of northern Argentina's great Chaco plain, travelling in two high-wheeled springless carts each drawn by six mules. The great journey north towards the Pilcomayo took them over inhospitable areas with little water and through places where the Indians were still hostile to outsiders. Food was mainly rice and beef cut wafer-thin and dried, called *charqui*, rather like parchment; often the maggots had to be knocked off before it was boiled or ground into powder in a mortar.

After two weeks they sighted the Pilcomayo river. The welcome they received came not from an Indian, but from a Texan cowboy! John Fitzgerald was the last member of a group who had been granted a concession of land by the Argentine government. He was delighted and amazed to receive two English speakers, whose presence he also felt would help pacify the Matacos, and he was pleased to donate a small extension of land for Alfred and Colin to establish a mission. The Matacos at that time still wore feathers, painted their faces, and used bows and arrows for hunting and for the continual feuds between the different clans. They were also succumbing to the white man's diseases.

The physical needs of these people were obvious, as was the fact that they were becoming harassed by the encroaching Argentine settlers and their cattle. They were certainly not hostile to the presence of the missionaries; on the contrary, they welcomed them. This is reflected in the name given to the English missionaries— *wajchäs,* 'water tail', those who came from the other side of the water. In contrast, the name

Journey of exploration to the Pilcomayo

given to the Argentine settlers was *ahätäy,* derived from the word for 'devils' and reflecting the fact that they saw them as oppressors.

Whilst Alfred was settling amongst the Matacos of the Pilcomayo and establishing a new mission called San Andrés, Dorothy was dreaming of the day she would join him. So she left Rust's and took a period of training at Redcliffe College before offering to the South American Missionary Society. It was this organisation, founded in 1844 by Captain Allen Gardiner, R.N., that had sponsored Alfred.

Both Alfred's and Dorothy's adventurous spirit and vision must have seemed very alien to the parochial mentality of their Norfolk village, and one imagines it would have been difficult for their parents to understand since they had probably hardly ventured out of the county. Yet they seem to have accepted their decisions. Indeed, Alfred's brother David later left home to work with the Iranian Oil Company in Abadan, and his sister Olive, after training at the Radcliffe

Infirmary, also went as a nurse to Argentina.

Misión San Andrés

Amongst the buildings erected at the new mission, most striking was the brick-built church. The mastermind was missionary William Cecil Everitt. Although a man of extraordinary abilities, he found mastery of the Mataco language difficult and always spoke with a decided accent and in a mixture of Mataco, English and Spanish. Yet through his dedication and commitment to the cause of the Indian people, he found no problem in communicating. His oft quoted maxim *ayudar la gente* (help the people) was lived out in practical action and his ability as a master wheelwright was seen in the making of many carts. It was with awe that I used to watch as the red hot iron rim was placed around the spokes which were then douched with water before they had time to burn the wood and contracted to hold the whole wheel fixed and tight.

Everitt was an able builder and the church in San Andrés

San Andrés church built by Cecil Everitt

was probably his masterpiece in the Chaco. It bore the style of an English country church with chancel, nave and Lady chapel and was constructed in English-size burnt red brick. It even had a tower containing a circular hole in readiness for a clock promised by Fitzgerald, although the American's good intentions never materialised. This imposing church was destroyed by the flooding Pilcomayo in the 1980s and disappeared under the silt.

Henry Grubb assumed responsibility in San Andrés and undertook the work of translating the New Testament into Mataco with the brilliant and able help of early Indian convert, Alberto González. Grubb had taken his degree at Cambridge in engineering, yet always felt it would have been more useful to have read medicine. Among the Indians and the Argentine settlers he proved more than just a dispenser of basic medicines and was recognized by them as a doctor and focus of consultation for all medical needs. He also undertook a full programme of teaching adults and children.

Tobas fishing in Pilcomayo River

2
The Tobas!

PRIOR to Henry Grubb's move to San Andrés, the mission had been visited by members of the Toba tribe from the east and further downstream. The Tobas were a different ethnic group, taller than the Matacos, with different tattoo marks and a variant culture. Their language also belonged to a distinct linguistic family; it sounded unlike Mataco and was structured differently. They presented themselves in their traditional feathered headdresses with ostrich feathers around their ankles. The Matacos called them the Ostrich tribe and there were those who regarded them as almost a mythological people whose knees, like those of the ostrich, bent backwards!

The purpose of the Tobas' visit was to ask that they, too, might have a missionary presence amongst them. Their motives may have been mixed: their first concern was to have someone who could teach their children and attend the sick, and also to be a kind of 'shock absorber' between them and the new settlers who were moving into their traditional lands and forests. They also needed somebody to protect them from the still regular incursions of the military and the police.

However, there was a broader canvas. Eighty years earlier, the South American Missionary Society's founder, Captain Allen Gardiner, had sent a prophetic letter to the Toba chiefs promising to send two missionaries to them, who would learn their language and care for the sick (see Appendix 1).

Alfred was designated to respond to this new development, a far cry from the village school, Allen's Garage in Cromer, and crabs and boats on the East Runton beach! In 1930,

Alfred and colleague Alec Sanderson mounted their mules and with their goods in big carts set off eastwards following the course of the River Pilcomayo to the land of the Tobas.

No roads existed, just cuttings through the forest. Large trunks were left two feet high, which had to be negotiated under the axles of the great two-wheelers. The carts had also to be carefully loaded. I have seen carts badly loaded with the imbalance of either too much weight for the mule in the shafts or the animal lifted off the ground if the cart pitched backwards! When going through dry river beds it was necessary to have a rider with a lasso hitched to the back to hold the cart as there were no brakes and to offset the weight bearing down on the mule in the shafts when going downhill. Once this operation had been achieved, the rider had to move to the front of the cart and the six mules and hitch to the shaft to give an extra pull forwards uphill. Thick black cart grease had to be regularly wiped on the bush (axle) because the constant friction of metal on metal caused loud screeching and quick wear. Wheels also had to be regularly soaked to keep the wooden spokes firmly in place.

A search for expression

The Tobas were located by the Pilcomayo just at the point where it is cut by the Tropic of Capricorn. The place was called Sombrero Negro (Black Hat), probably because one of the well-known chiefs had been presented with one whilst working at the sugar plantations where the Indians were employed as cheap labour to harvest the cane.

On arrival, Alfred found himself surrounded by inquisitive

and fascinated people, all the children completely naked, curiously watching every move, women with intricate facial tattoo marks, men with painted faces and feathers—all in contrast even with the Matacos in Misión Chaqueña, many of whom had already adopted European dress and short hair. Bows and arrows were the norm for hunting, so Alfred's Winchester 22 and double-barrelled twelve-bore stood in stark contrast.

The Tobas were proud to have attracted the presence of a white foreigner. He was referred to initially as *Cadeta*, 'our father'; then as his presence became more familiar, he was referred to as *Cadacaya*, 'our other', and later as *Cadanoguiagaua*, 'our suckling companion'. Alfred always appreciated the sequence of these names as a kind of gradual and closer identification with these people.

As Alfred walked around the Toba village, notebook in hand, taking down basic details of the language, he was heckled teasingly with the shouts *Kalak kadakataka*—"our words are difficult". "They certainly are!" he must have mused. His time would have been spent pointing at objects which were part of their daily lives and finding out the corresponding words, such as *niyac* for fish, *map* for the algarroba carob bean (an Indian staple), *neue* for headdress, *ñachi* for river.

This was a language that had never been reduced to writing. For the Tobas here was the first white man ever to be interested in the fact that they even had a language, with its peculiar grammar and some words used exclusively by men and others solely by women. It was one thing to find names

Committee of Tobas requesting a mission to be started among them, with my father

and nouns, it was going to prove quite another to find the language to describe mythological and spiritual concepts.

Whilst Alfred battled in the forests, making his first attempts at this language, Dorothy continued at Rust's and then at Redcliffe College, anticipating that some day she would join him. Yet from her North Norfolk village background she could hardly have imagined what type of life awaited her in remote Northern Argentina, the only clues coming from descriptions afforded by Alfred in his sporadic letters, as and when an outside visitor arrived in Sombrero Negro or the Toba 'mail boy' was sent to the railhead to take post.

Apart from the time given to learn the language and gradually absorb, understand and in some measure identify with the culture, a survey was undertaken as to where to locate the homes and centre for the mission amongst the Tobas. For the first weeks and months Alfred and his colleague lived in a tent. They slept on roughly-made beds under a net to protect from the swarms of mosquitoes and the vinchuca, a 'bed bug' of the Reduviid family which lives on the blood taken from its victims. The full menace of this insect, apart from the irritation caused by the bite, was not known or understood until investigators Carlos Chagas and Salvador Mazza undertook research and identified the illness incubated and transmitted by the vinchuca which caused tiredness, lethargy and ultimately heart problems.

The disease became popularly known as *Chagas*. Recent studies have indicated that 60 per cent of people living in the Chaco area carry it. I have been diagnosed as *Chagas* positive, but have been assured by my friend Dr Michael Patterson that I will probably live to the age of 90 and die of 'flu! Maybe its danger has been overrated, although I have seen many apparently healthy people die suddenly, their deaths attributed to *Chagas*. Latterly, fumigating campaigns have been organised and it has been amazing to see Nido milk tins full of dead vinchucas taken from Indian huts.

During his constant open contact with the Tobas, Alfred gradually collected and collated sufficient words to preach his first sermon on March 22, 1931. He was, however, somewhat mystified when his words about Jesus and his death on the cross were met with laughter. To the Tobas, matters causing suffering or accident produce not pity but hilarity. I remember hearing a woman relate the story of how an Argentine settler attempted to cross the river with his cattle and was swept away and drowned. His body was later found further downstream, chewed up by hungry piranhas. The woman told the story with great delight, each detail punctuated by prolonged

Toba home in the shade of an algarrobo tree

laughter. In day-to-day life a trip or an accidental bumping of the head prompts a snigger.

Incarnating the Gospel

Alongside hands-on language learning and cultural orientation, Alfred was also involved in the preparation and building of more permanent dwellings. Unlike modern-day mission partners, he had no linguistic studies and much less any course in social anthropology or missiology. Yet he seems to have been endowed with a depth of sanctified common sense in his approach to his work and his identification with the Indians. His deep sense of commitment and even his shyness—in the Church Army he was excused speaking at the open-air meetings in Hyde Park corner—afforded him the right approach to his ministry among the Tobas.

He lived with them and shared many of their games and dances in order to gain the right to share the Christian faith. Instead of presenting to them something superficial which ignored their culture and customs, he sought to bring Christianity to them in depth on their terms and in their language, accepting their understanding and world-view, but demonstrating and teaching changes that could remove suffering and fear. Culture is important, but not sacrosanct. He challenged the custom of burying the terminally ill whilst still alive, the killing of a twin child, and widows being made to shave their heads and sit isolated in a small brushwood hut for weeks after their husband's death.

In two years with the Tobas, Alfred had mastered sufficient of the language to hold a conversation and teach the children

Toba men preparing 'aloja' (beer)

and adults in school. He was an accepted person in the Indian community life, often seen as the arbiter in inter-tribal fighting and internal fights between groups of women, sadly a regular phenomenon! He was often called on to protect Indian rights from encroaching Argentine settlers. His building work was evidenced by the permanent adobe dwellings with split palm roofs now nestling under the shady algarrobo trees.

Much had been accomplished in those short years, and in 1932 Alfred returned to the UK for a well-earned leave. No doubt about the highlight of this time in England—his engagement to Dorothy! I was always intrigued that a photograph of Beeston Regis Church on the Norfolk coast was placed at the beginning of an album of black and white photographs of life amongst the Tobas. It was there that Alfred and Dorothy became engaged!

The Chaco War

Alfred returned to Argentina in 1933. His sister Olive had by now come to work at the Toba mission and was able to provide a feminine dimension in what had been until then a completely male environment. Olive helped pave the way for Dorothy's arrival, and as a nurse provided the necessary medical help for the Indians.

Alfred arrived to find the Chaco War, a conflict between Paraguay and Bolivia over the question of possible oil in the area, at its height. The battle frontier was just over the river from the mission and the Toba settlement, and many vicious battles were fought there. The Bolivian soldiers who had come down from the cold highlands suffered greatly in the hot dry forests and many deserted, handing themselves over to the Argentine military authorities who had established a reception centre for them at the new railhead known as Ingeniero Juárez, about 60 miles to the south of the River Pilcomayo.

The Paraguayan soldiers had a reputation for being completely ruthless, adept with knives in hand-to-hand fighting and known for shooting all in sight. Many Indians were killed for merely walking on to the riverbank on the Paraguayan side while fishing, quite unaware of the new political boundaries being established. One evening later in the war, Alfred and Dorothy were strolling by the river and had to scurry hastily back as Paraguayan soldiers opened fire on the Indians fishing, shots splashing the water nearby. A letter of complaint was sent to the Paraguayan officer in charge, whose reply was blatantly aggressive. "Next time", he said, "I'll order my men to shoot to kill."

Nor could the Indians often tell the difference between Paraguayan and Bolivian soldiers, and many Bolivian deserters sought the help of Indians to cross the river only to be drowned in revenge for actions committed by the Paraguayan soldiers. Indians who guided soldiers across the river were often paid in silver spurs, knives, horsewhips or revolvers, and many would appear in army uniforms that they had come by. I remember as a young boy one in particular nicknamed 'Presidente' who wore an army greatcoat complete with brass buttons.

In the course of the war, the land over the river which had been Bolivia became part of Paraguay, a decision made by the six Latin American Presidents acting as arbitrators.

3

Together at last!

ALFRED felt that such an auspicious and important occasion as his marriage should be shared in the first place with Choliqui, the great chief of the Toba nation. But when Alfred told him the exciting news the chief remained silent for a few moments before replying: "Do you want to buy a pumpkin?" It seemed he was not too concerned or apparently interested in Alfred's wedding plans! Tobas generally show little emotion or expression of surprise.

In spite of Choliqui's indifference, Dorothy would leave her Norfolk village, make the voyage to Buenos Aires and then the extended train journey to Ingeniero Juárez for her wedding. After her studies at Redcliffe College, a place of training for women candidates who offered for overseas missionary service—where discipline was demanding and a uniform worn—she prepared for her journey on a cargo vessel, packing carefully in her luggage the wedding dress she had made and the shoes to go with it. Alfred, having acquainted himself thoroughly with the Toba culture and identified himself with the Tobas, wanted to celebrate his wedding amongst them, so he and Dorothy decided they should marry in Argentina at the mission, Misión El Toba.

The bridal train

Dorothy arrived in Buenos Aires on July 5, 1934, and after a few days embarked on the five-day train journey to Ingeniero Juárez, and from there by truck to Misión El Toba. She was met on the platform of Juárez station by Alfred, for whom last hour or so must have seemed an eternity. The line that crosses the centre of the Argentine Chaco linking the city of Formosa with the small town of Embarcación had just been completed and at that time was the straightest section of railway track in the world. The wood-burning steam engine's headlamp could be seen as a small speck in the distance long before the train arrived! The platform was strewn with sleeping would-be passengers, while the waft of cheap perfume was evident as both young and old came out at whatever time the train arrived. It was the event of the week, the opportunity to see and be seen.

The train thundered in, moving unsteadily from side to side, the cowcatcher nosing to left, then right, ash and cinders strewn on to the platform, following the engine a convoy of goods wagons and then the second class carriages and sleeper. The train screeched to a halt, the chickens in their cage under the dining car covered in dust, passengers hanging out of the windows excitedly preparing to disembark whilst others in drunken unconsciousness slept on. The aroma of perfume was replaced by the smell of stinking toilets and hot metal as the brakes were applied. It was a typical scene from a western film, all so apt for this one horse town. Ingeniero Juárez was certainly a long way from Cromer station where Dorothy's journey had started!

Alfred and Dorothy trundled their luggage over the railway lines, since the town had grown up on the opposite side to the one anticipated by the early surveyors and planners. The hotel was about 200 yards away, a wooden ramshackle building owned by a Catalan surnamed Domenech who had a chronic sniffle and regularly wiped his nose on the dishcloth as he shuffled back and forth bringing consommé, prepared on the outside wooden stove, to the dining table.

Early next day Lisandro Ovejero, the registrar and JP for the settlement of Ingeniero Juárez, was in his wooden office, a two-roomed cast-off prefabricated hut provided by the railway's builders after the line was completed. The marriage register was on the shelf alongside the register of cattle brands and earmarks! Alfred and his bride Dorothy stood on a puma skin as Ovejero asked the questions. Missionaries Henry Grubb and Alfred Tompkins were the witnesses.

Dorothy spoke no Spanish, but Alfred had prepared her with the answers, telling her that when he nudged her she should simply say *"Sí"*. When the moment came, such was her excitement she blurted out *"Sí ... sí"*!

The marriage certificate registers that Alfred had been resident in the country for seven years and Dorothy 14 days, certainly the most momentous 14 days in her life. So many new experiences in such a short time, yet these were just a preliminary of what was to follow.

After the civil ceremony in the little Registry Office, Alfred and Dorothy travelled northwards from Juárez to Sombrero Negro by the Pilcomayo river in an ancient Ford truck, accompanied by Tompkins, Grubb, Canon Bevis and others. In 1934 the 'road' was just a track through the forest, used by the occasional mule-drawn cart supplying the isolated stores, or a troop of cattle goaded on by the local *chaqueños* on their horses.

These Chaco cowboys use protective *guardamontes* and

wear *coletos* to guard them from the cacti and thorns as they crash through the forest to bring a wandering steer back to the road and to the rest of the cattle that are following the sound of a horn blown by a child mounted on a horse leading the troop.

The first stop was Pozo de Maza, a halfway post between the railroad and the river. Here a breakfast was served at the *boliche* owned by Carlos Lávaque. Never before had the store witnessed such a group of customers and the event was always remembered by Lávaque's daughter who continued to run the place.

Many such stores were owned by Arab merchants who had immigrated to Argentina to seek their fortunes. I met an old Iraqi whose family had travelled out steerage on the ill-fated *Titanic*, and had a miraculous rescue. He could hardly remember the name of the ship on which he had left Southampton and seemed unaware of the significance of the story he was telling me.

There being no phone or radio communication, the Tobas and missionaries waiting in Misión El Toba had no clear idea of the time of arrival of the newlyweds and their entourage, so the Indians continued their normal activities. The younger men were fully involved in a game of native hockey, where there seemed to be no boundaries and rough play swept right through the village, the only observable objective being to place the wooden 'ball' into a pile of bushes at each end of the cleared ground.

There was no rule to say how high you could lift your stick, so many players lost eyes and suffered broken legs. They played in loincloths with feathers around their ankles, no

Hockey game in full swing

shoes and with long hair flowing. As an incentive to greater endeavours in the game and to foster and encourage speed, the players would stab themselves with sharp bone from the knuckles of the ostrich. Blood would stream from these wounds, along with sweat mixed with a great covering of dust.

At the height of this game Alfred and Dorothy arrived. The game of hockey ended, they duly transferred from the Ford to a four-wheeler which

Hockey player Mauricio, bleeding with ostrich bone

My mother's wedding day

in large letters announced in English 'Ray of Sunshine Carrier'. Before Dorothy left England, friends and members of the South American Missionary Society had encouraged her by saying that she would be a ray of sunshine to the mainly bachelor missionary establishment.

The reckless hockey teams pushed her at breakneck speed the two kilometres to the mission where she would see for the first time the adobe house that Alfred had built with its corrugated metal roof covered with cane to try to protect it from the excessive heat—sometimes reaching 45°. For her relief and support, Alfred's sister Olive was at the mission, and with her two years' experience was able to offer some help and orientation. Others who had come to the wedding were the Revd Alfred Tompkins with his wife Gertrude and son Norman, Alfred Cox, William White, and Archdeacon

Guy Bevis from Buenos Aires, who had travelled from there with Dorothy. Norman Tompkins was about ten years old at the time of the wedding. Years later, after a successful career with Dunlop and living in the West Indies, Peru and Spain, he returned to Argentina with his wife Emily and their daughters Marina, Mónica and Cora. It is fascinating to see

They had never seen a "white" bride before

how the wheels turn. Mónica was one of the first women candidates for the ordained ministry and I had the privilege of ordaining her deacon in St John's Cathedral in Buenos Aires. At the time of writing she is responsible for the congregation in the city of Rosario. Norman and his brothers Francis and John all went to school at St George's College in Quilmes in Buenos Aires. Francis followed in his father's footsteps and served with his wife Jean as a missionary in Misión Chaqueña amongst the Matacos. For a time he was responsible for all the Anglican Missions in the Chaco. Like his brothers, he had learnt Mataco as a boy and was well acquainted with the people who, catching on to his mother's pet name for him as a baby, called him '*Sanbim*' (their transliteration of Sunbeam).

The Tompkins, Leake, Everitt and Grubb families who contributed many decades to missionary service amongst the Mataco and Toba Indians were commemorated in August 2002 by the dedication of engraved wooden plaques placed in the church at Misión Chaqueña and the presentation of a memorial bell. I had the privilege of dedicating the bell before it was hung on a nearby algarrobo tree, as well as the beautifully engraved quebracho plaques which had been commissioned by Alec Deane, a former Irish-Argentine missionary and now director of Siwok Crafts, a charity which encourages the carving and marketing of beautiful wooden handicrafts made by the men of Misión Chaqueña. All this took place at a special service which coincided with the presentation of the completed Bible in Mataco (now called Wichi). This mammoth task, following in the steps of Richard Hunt and Henry Grubb, was undertaken by Robert Lunt and a team of Wichi helpers. This translation is a momentous milestone in the life of the Anglican Wichi church, placing in the hands of that people the Word of God in their own language.

A unique wedding

The wedding service was unique in that the majority of the congregation were Tobas, with a small number of English missionaries; the main part of the service was in Toba with only some sections in English. Alfred wore a suit and tie and Dorothy the wedding dress she had made whilst still in East Runton. As one looks back from these less formal times and pores over the photographs, it all seems so incongruous and a complete contrast to the rest of the congregation, many wearing just loincloths, children naked, men with feather headdresses, the tattooed faces of the women, their heads crowned with bright headscarves brought back from the sugar cane plantations, young mothers suckling their babies, dogs wandering in and out and occasionally fighting, parakeets screeching from their nests in the algarrobo trees outside the church. Against this background, Bill Price pedalled the bellows of the small harmonium and translated into Toba whilst the Revd Alfred Tompkins conducted the service.

The colourful wedding was followed by a feast for all. Steers were slaughtered and a big stew prepared. Then, in contrast to the native hockey game, a football match was held, Alfred donating a leather ball and shirts for the players!

Alfred and Dorothy did not travel anywhere for their honeymoon and remained in Misión El Toba, living in the house that Alfred had built, a simple two-roomed structure with a porch and a small room that served as a bathroom. The kitchen was a separate building because of the heat from the wooden fire, while the toilet was a long-drop about 50 metres from the house, a simple wooden shed that looked like a sentinel's hut. This facility was shared with other missionary staff and, to avoid the annoyance of walking the 50 metres only to find it engaged, there was a signal that had to be turned to white to indicate 'all clear'. Red signalled 'engaged'!

However, sometimes people forgot to turn the signal when entering or leaving! A satirical author writing a book about long-drops entitled *The Specialist* made the sparkling suggestion that the woodpile should be placed between the kitchen and the lavatory since one could always pick up a log of wood on one's way back. Or else, if as often happened, there was a crowd of people standing around, one could pretend just to be fetching firewood and so save the embarrassment of being a public spectacle.

Dorothy took a full part in the continuing missionary work amongst the Tobas. Her first task was to learn the language, and she soon picked up a working knowledge to cover activities in the house and enough to help her with reading classes for the older girls. Her Spanish was always elementary. She had a wonderful sense of humour and Alfred commented that she made her needs known and communicated through "signs and wonders"!

She had a great fear of insects and snakes, but was very brave in facing many different situations. She once almost picked up a rattlesnake which was coiled up with some rope. One morning she entered the kitchen to see an opossum's snout sticking over one side of a large saucepan and the tail hanging over the other side. She found facing accidents and being called upon to provide first aid difficult, and yet often when Alfred was away she was resorted to by Indians who had suffered injury whilst chopping wood or were victims of deep piranha bites when chunks of flesh were literally torn out by razor-sharp teeth.

A young Toba was spearing fish, and to prevent the fish

slipping off his spear, which had no barb, he dived to secure it. Unfortunately the fish slid from the spear, and as the young man dived into the water attempting to secure his catch, a piranha swam up and bit his face, taking away part of his cheek. In Alfred's absence, Dorothy was asked to attend the victim. His face eventually healed, leaving a massive scar which he kept covered with a rag. On another occasion, I remember a Toba fisherman having a large part of his stomach gouged out. The piranha are merciless, their teeth as sharp as razor blades, and Indian women would keep a set in their sewing bags, using them to cut string and cotton.

My father with Toba youngsters dancing

My parents after their wedding

4

A great place to start life

ALFRED and Dorothy lived those early months together in their adobe house in the shade of the algarrobo trees, about 150 metres from the River Pilcomayo opposite Paraguay, right on the Tropic of Capricorn. The Chaco War apart, all was quiet, except for the constant chattering of the small green parakeets and the deafening shrill of the railway beetles (cicadas).

Toba youth

Life on the Toba mission station took on a regular rhythm dictated by the ringing of the bell hung high on a branch of an algarrobo tree. Long before dawn it sounded for morning prayers and Toba men, followed by their womenfolk, would wind their way along the well-marked paths to the large cane-built palm-roofed church.

Activities always started early in the Indian villages. It was imperative to ensure the dying embers of the fire were brought together and rekindled. Matches were not easily available and starting a fire with sticks took a while, so the alternative was the embarrassment of asking your neighbour for some embers.

The morning prayer service was followed by another bell which announced the start of school. Children, some in rags, others wearing almost nothing, would come rushing from every direction, all willing attenders. School started with the raising of the Argentine flag, an event which must have been very puzzling to the children, but a good public relations exercise *vis-à-vis* the military authorities who occasionally appeared in this remote area to keep an eye on the war and also be ready to suffocate what might be seen as signs of an Indian uprising. Once inside the school building each child was provided with a slate and pencil, and basic teaching in reading and arithmetic was given. Alfred would be fully involved in this work with the boys and Dorothy would follow with the girls.

The bell was rung once again, this time signifying that the *botica* was open. This was a basic first-aid centre and Alfred and his sister Olive would attend all who came for medical help. Ailments could be piranha bites, snake bites and all

Toba youths in for a swim

manner of undetermined aches and pains which the Tobas would describe using the missionary's body, poking different parts to indicate the location of the pain.

Basic medicines were prepared there. Tuberculosis was chronic in the area so 'cough mixture' was in great demand. Among other favourite treatments were the colourful potassium permanganate crystals, which before anti-venom was available were used for snakebite. After a tourniquet had been applied, the area of the teeth marks was incised and encouraged to bleed to help remove the poison, and then permanganate was used to disinfect the wound. Riding accidents were frequent as were wounds caused by kicks from horse or mule. I well recall my father making me witness him attending to some of these accidents.

Teeth were extracted in the *botica* without anaesthetic, and one would regularly hear screams as a molar came out. The patient would then be seen standing outside, spitting and examining the extracted tooth.

Argentine settlers also came to the *botica,* but the Indians resented them being cared for as they were seen as the oppressors and the cause of conflict and trouble.

Many wounds were serious and the care was basic. Alfred often regretted he had not been able to undertake some basic training which would have enabled him to stitch wounds or give some form of anaesthetic before removing teeth.

But at that time it was the only help available and was much appreciated. One of Alfred's colleagues and co-founder of the Toba mission was Colin Smith. He was always referred to as "doctor", although he had not completed his final medical exams. He was located in San Andrés and was occasionally resorted to in particularly difficult cases. He became well known in later years for his attention to patients with Malta fever, although healing must often have been more psychological than physical since it is doubtful whether the large number of bottles filled with medicine could have been as effective as claimed! For animist Indians and superstitious Argentine settlers, perhaps the fact that they "felt better" with the remedies given was success in itself.

I remember one particularly tragic accident. An Argentine cowboy was rounding up cattle on the Paraguayan side of the river. He was naked and the horse was wet, having just come out of the water. As it jumped a small bank, the rider slid off onto a stick he was using for the round-up. The stick penetrated his backside causing internal injuries. He was treated on the mission, then transferred to Ingeniero Juárez and sent by train to Formosa, but sadly he died on the journey.

"A son born to Mrs W.A. Leake at 3 am"

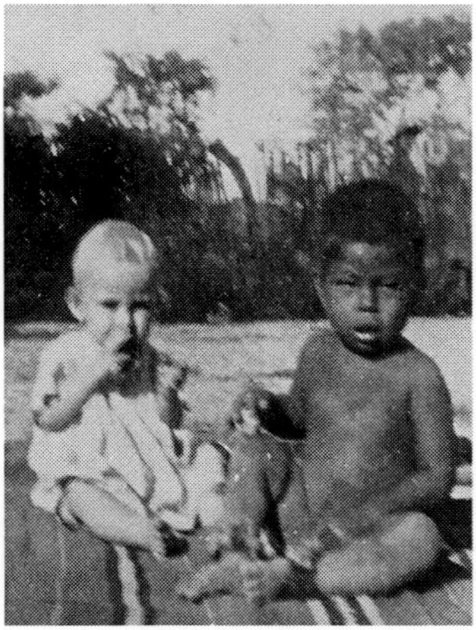

So runs the formal, succinct comment in Alfred's handwriting in the Toba mission station diary. Just as Alfred, no doubt with Dorothy's complete approval, had decided that their wedding should be celebrated within the Toba community, so too they felt that the birth of their children and family life should be

With Naldi, my first Toba friend

My father (r) with Colin Smith and Juan Rumalda

should be lived out within the context of the Toba world.

So I was born in an adobe house, my mother being assisted and accompanied by my Auntie Olive. On 30 June the diary continues with the comment: "Baby taken out for first outing in pram with an escort of over 80 children!" I was certainly the first white European child they had ever seen.

At birth, I had no hair and rather protruding ears and so was immediately named *Quitelaic* (Large Ears). The Indians have always been keen observers of physical characteristics and human behaviour and quick to affix an appropriate nickname. Henry Grubb was called *Techinhas*, Iron Eyes, as he wore metal-rimmed glasses. William Everitt, the master carpenter, was *Nihiyä* and *Mukuk*, the name of a small insect which has the ability to cut branches from trees by apparently circling them constantly till they fall. Olive Leake (later Grubb) was called *Jadiyocole*, the quiet unseen one. William Underwood, who never gave warning of travel and visits, was *Nitoyates*, the unannounced

My first horse ride with mother and Cristina!

one. Alfred Tompkins was *Alfredo Tomagadaic* to the Tobas, that is, Alfred the Red, because of his complexion. He was known by the Matacos as *Kato T'unho*, Stiff Elbow, a name given after some had observed that when serving in the mission store he would put just enough sugar or flour on the plate of the weighing machine to complete the kilo! An unfair name since Alfred Tompkins was most generous!

More recent missionaries also had their local Indian names. Patrick Harris was *Käjyentes*, the one who makes us happy, Robert Lunt was *Fwalalä*, the name of a small red bird (the vermilion flycatcher), either because of his complexion and red hair or because he often wore a red pullover.

The Indians themselves also had colourful names such as Donkey's Ears, Burnt Bottom, Tailless Toad, Black Shoulder, Captive One, Non-Swimmer, Armadillo Head and many others.

My early days

No doubt in line with the thinking of the time, I was not brought up on demand

Choliqui, Toba Indian Chief

feeding, unlike all the Toba babies whose first years of life were spent in a sling never more than an inch away from a breast always well supplied with mother's milk. My mother fed me at fixed times. During the intervening periods I cried a lot, and so to distance the house from the yelling child a small shelter was built about 20 metres away, and I was placed there inside what was a meat , safe as protection from flies, mosquitoes and other insects that might be around. My mother was harangued as being uncaring of her firstborn by the Indian women as they passed the house to fetch water from the river. I came to no harm, however, and grew up greatly loved and healthy in what many would have regarded as an unfavourably hot and inhospitable environment.

With Ualcayis the kitchen boy

Snail mail

The Toba Mission Diary recalls the normal activities and events in the Toba village. The sending and receiving of mail, for example, is often commented on. In an age when communication has become so accelerated and noteworthy events are known all over the world within minutes, it is difficult to believe that letters could take up to three months to arrive from Europe. Fetching them from the railhead in Ingeniero Juárez was a return journey of three to four days on a horse, and I recall that after such a journey sometimes there would be just a packet of very outdated newspapers.

Fishing expeditions

The school was often closed when the village went off on a fishing expedition. These were announced by the chief or some leader with a loud shout which was the call to all men

Roasting fish after a successful fishing expedition

and boys to take up their fishing nets, repeat the call and make for the river. Women and children often followed and the village emptied except for some caretaker elderly folks. Besides their nets, many would carry a smouldering piece of wood to start a fire for roasting fish.

There were basically two main styles of fishing with nets, depending on the depth of the river: in deep water the poles supporting the net were joined at both ends and the fisherman dived for fish. I never cease to marvel at the Indians' ability to identify the presence of fish, even its type and size, by the smallest movement and formation on the surface of the water. The most popular method, when circumstances allowed, was to select a section of the river where it was shallow. The fishermen would stand across the river, shoulder to shoulder, holding nets in scissor formation. These, splayed out, formed a network across the river. Other men with long poles would work their way upstream from a distance of about 100 metres, hitting and splashing the water with their poles, thus frightening the fish and driving them towards the netbearers. As the men caught the fish these would be strung like a skirt around the waist. The 'beaters' would then move down the river again and repeat the exercise. The Indians revelled in this type of community activity. It was certainly not seen as work, but as a lifestyle, although it was not without its dangers from piranha bites or stepping on the barb of a catfish or stingray—dangers which so concerned my mother that my own fishing was limited to sitting on the bank with hook and line.

A third option was spearing fish in shallow water. A fourth, and once the cause of many fights between tribal groups, was to build a trap across the river when the fish were making their way upstream to their spawning areas. These traps were made by placing poles closely alongside each other, stuck upright in the riverbed. This formed a total barrier for the fish which were then easily caught in nets as they desperately battled to swim upstream against the current. Wounds on fish that did manage to get through the trap were evidence that such a trap existed downstream and this became cause for feuds between the Tobas and the Chunupí who lived further downstream.

As well as being the source of much needed and healthy food, the River Pilcomayo was the focal point for family outings. The man would walk to the river, followed by his wife with a large earthen water pot on her back suspended by a cord from her forehead and maybe carrying a bucket bought at the sugar cane plantation store. She might also bear a baby in a sling as well as an older child on her shoulder, while dogs and other children followed along.

Time at the river would be spent cooling off in the extreme heat. A small bowl-sized hole would be dug in which the still water would cause the silt to settle, thus providing cleaner water for washing clothes. This was undertaken with characteristic beating of the dirty laundry, the sound echoing back from the opposite bank. Once all was completed, the family would return home, a large leaf from the castor oil plant floating on the water in the bucket or stuffed in the neck of the water pot to prevent spillage. It is from this plant that the infamous ricin is made.

The river also became the playground for the boys who would enjoy a game styled on 'tag'. This caused great merriment and laughter, involving chases along the banks and diving into the river. In many cases nothing was worn except a G-string and bodies would glisten in the sun. Girls played in the river, often forming a circle or else standing opposite each other, and with rhythmic motions bounce up and down in the water and with a movement of the elbows in unison make a resounding echoing noise.

Nannies

As I grew up amongst the Indians, my parents were fully involved in the activities of the mission and always at the beck and call of the Tobas. My mother commended me to the care of two ‘nannies’, one Cajecholi and the other Nano’ole, who looked after me during the hours that she was involved in teaching activities and other meetings with the Indian women. I grew up, therefore, learning Toba as my first language, and I suppose one could say that my first concepts were from the Indian culture. The first word that I formed was *coic,* which means tobacco, much to the bewilderment of my grandmother when with my parents I made my first visit to the UK in 1938 at the age of three! My two nannies were always expectant of some gift when I visited them as a grown-up, and were happy when I provided them with some sugar and *yerba* (herbal tea) or a length of cloth.

Fun and games

One of my earliest games was *cadi*, which was a kind of hunting sling which was swung and thrown to the ground and ended coiled up with the other players’ slings, and they in turn threw theirs down in the same place. I don’t recall the actual dynamics of the game, but it was related to who threw first and whose *cadi* became coiled with another when lifted off the ground.

Using a catapult to shoot parakeets and other birds for food was very much part of early memories. Every Indian boy,

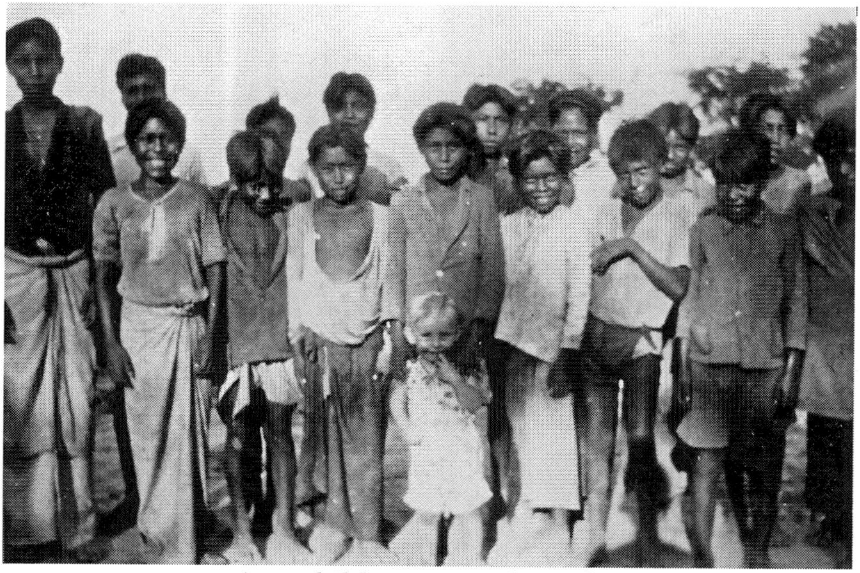

As a child amongst the Tobas

even if he wore no clothes, carried a small string bag with round marbles of mud made from the clay by the river. The elastic rubber for the catapult was available in the store in Sombrero Negro or from the mission store and was sold by the metre. In later years we also used pieces of discarded inner tubes. Some catapults were made from a forked stick, whilst boys with greater ability hooked the ends of the elastic to their thumb and forefinger and shot direct.

The traditional game of native hockey was no longer played when I was a boy and had been replaced by football. The Tobas are adept footballers, and the area would be good for talent-spotting for professional teams! Wrestling was a common activity, and this often took place in response to a challenge of *"Am Jajagaini"* (I will throw you down) as a last resort when a verbal argument no longer served to resolve a matter.

Mounting pastimes

To have enjoyed many such outdoor pursuits in England I would have had to belong to the privileged classes. Yet these were natural activities available almost 'for free' in the open spaces, the Chaco forests and grasslands. My mother often said, "We do not have much money, but we do see life!"

On one of my early birthdays a colleague of my father, Bill Price, gave me a donkey's foal. It was tied outside our home with a pink ribbon round its neck and was named Pixie. She went on to produce many offspring and descendants. Our home and the surrounding villages were inhabited by troops of donkeys, and great commotions were caused by stallions chasing rivals through the villages. Hooves and dust would fly, and there would be bleeding wounds on their necks. These hardy animals rarely succumbed to illness and were able to live on the basic thorny vegetation. I remember making a deal with an Argentine settler who noticed the particular colouring of one of my donkeys and wanted it to place with

Toba with a toucan headdress

his mares to produce mules. I felt I had done a good deal when he gave me in exchange a young piebald mare.

Donkey ride under care of Degan

My early riding experience was on donkeys, initially led round by an Indian. A further development was harnessing the donkey to a small cart and undertaking expeditions to the river to collect driftwood for my mother's kitchen fire. On one occasion the donkey ran amok and my sister Cristina, who had been delegated to lead it, ran off and climbed up a tree in terror!

From donkeys I advanced to horses. My first mare was bought from a Mataco who lived further upstream. Like its donkey counterparts, it reproduced regularly and at one point I was the proud owner of five horses.

I used the type of saddlery of the Argentine cowboy settlers. This was made up of four square woven horse mats with intricate patterns and covered with a leather *carona* which kept the saddle from slipping. The saddle was placed on the *carona* and held tight with the cinch. It was then covered with two or three sheepskins which in turn were covered with a piece of thin tanned skin, and all held on with a further smaller cinch. A folded poncho was also laid across the front of the saddle.

The rider carried his lasso resting on the rump of the horse and fastened to the back of the saddle, which basic belongings were packed in a pair of red woven saddlebags. The halter was ornamentally woven in crude leather. The bit with the reins often had a mouthpiece which jangled as the horse turned it over with its tongue. My own equipment was not up to the standard described, but I was nicknamed *Gaucho sin vacas*, 'Cowboy with no cows'.

With my first horse

as the horse turned it over with its tongue. My own equipment was not up to the standard described, but I was nicknamed *Gaucho sin vacas*, 'Cowboy with no cows'.

I recall a near serious accident once when I was riding bareback from the river after taking a horse to drink. No sooner had I mounted, than it set off home at a gallop. I narrowly missed hitting my knee on the gatepost and after 50

My sisters Cristina and Dorothy with my mare and foal and Cristina with a fox

or so metres I came off. I must have fainted for a few seconds and came to come to lying under the horse with its turned head looking down at me.

Many happy days were spent with my Toba friend José Florentín, riding and shooting. My father had a double-barrelled twelve-bore and also a Winchester 22, and our target was mainly a type of small brown pheasant.

As a young boy standing by an algarrobo trunk

5
Moving to another kind of education

MY HAPPY and wonderful free life in the forests of the Chaco was interrupted by the need for more structured schooling. My mother had helped me with early basics, and then for the birth of my younger sister Dorothy in 1943 we went to the sugar plantations of La Esperanza. My aunt Olive had returned to England, and it was arranged that my mother would be cared for at the hospital in the town of San Pedro de Jujuy. This afforded the opportunity for my sister Cristina and me to have some lessons and be tutored by Daisy Easdale, daughter of Baptist missionary Thomas Easdale. Daisy was an excellent teacher and a gifted artist; she took on this challenge with great creativity and seriousness, organising us as though we were a full-sized prep school, with a sports day and prizegiving at which my parents would sit and watch!

We remained in La Esperanza for about six months during which time Dorothy was born. She had a clear V-shaped birthmark on her forehead which soon disappeared but was seen as a positive omen of victory in the Second World War. Cristina and I benefited from our initial studies and I still treasure after all these years my first exercise book. I have often used it in sermons to illustrate the need to move on: what may have been good and excellent at one point in life needs to be improved.

One of the big events during our time there was the purchase of our first car, a second-hand saloon model Ford A with a canvas hood. All journeys until this time had been by horse or mule-drawn carts. My mother, sisters and I remained in La

Esperanza whilst my father, accompanied by Thomas Easdale, made the journey in the car to Misión El Toba. This was an opportunity to get back to see the Tobas and also to give my father a feel of the car before the long journey home with the family.

His early work and experiences at Allen's Garage in Cromer would stand the mission work in good stead as he undertook all maintenance and repairs. Deeply concerned for his new acquisition, he recorded that Mr Easdale hit a number of tree stumps, and when he remonstrated with him, Easdale replied, "You complain about all the ones I hit, but say nothing commendable about all the ones I miss."

We had to carry practically everything, from the basic puncture repair kit (with which we vulcanised the inner tube) to a spare axle. I recall on one occasion during the war when there was a shortage of rubber and inner tubes and tyres were difficult to come by, that my father filled old tyres with grass, but because of the friction caused, the tyre caught fire by spontaneous combustion.

The Ford A did not have a petrol pump, petrol being fed by gravity from the tank which was in front of the steering wheel. The supports for the windscreen rested at each end of the tank and due to the constant bumps and vibrations these often cracked. I recall my father's horror as he watched the supports being welded, with only some wet sacks wrapped around the tank ends as a precaution against explosion or fire!

My father built a reputation as an expert driver, capable, according to the Arab store man, of driving through water when it was chest deep!

School in Buenos Aires: once a year!

I don't recall whether I went willingly or unwillingly to school. Looking back, I think I was ill-prepared for leaving the family and all that was so familiar in the Toba village to travel the 1,000 miles or so to the city of Buenos Aires. My only friends had been the Toba children, my languages Toba and English at home. Spanish was a foreign language since we had little contact with Spanish speakers, and this resulted in my having to repeat first grade in Buenos Aires.

Owing to the distance and difficulties of travel, I would leave for school in early March and not return home until the end of the school year in November. When I speak to children, I often tell them that as a boy I only went to school once a year—and then add that I only went home once a year too! Journeys to and from school were memorable, full of joy and excitement or sadness and foreboding, depending on which direction I was going!

They often started by mule cart, as weather conditions made it impossible to travel in the Ford. Days before the journey, my father would arrange for the cartwheels to be soaked in the river to tighten the wooden spokes, as often the extended hot weather would dry out the wooden wheels and the spokes became loose.

The mules, which ran free to forage in the forest, had to be caught and brought in. This was relatively easy as they had a regular watering hole or point on the river where they would drink. However, sometimes owing to long periods of freedom they would be quite frisky and each had its particular customs. I remember one in particular which was nicknamed in Toba

'Untouchable Ears', who always had to be harnessed and chained in last, as once hooked up she had to be off.

Some of these were mules discarded from the sugar cane plantations and given to the Indians at the end of the harvest season. They always held a fascination for the Indian children, who had never seen horses shod. The cane fields area had stones, whilst the sandy Chaco forest made shoeing animals unnecessary.

Leaving the Toba mission was a colourful but sad affair, as I knew that I would not be seeing my parents, sisters and Indian friends for nine months. We would leave very early while it was still dark and cool. The nights preceding our departure were usually tearful. I felt sorry for myself at having to leave home, and only realised later in life that the heartbreak must have been equally strong for my parents who would not see their son for so long. He would live a life quite alien to the one spent amongst the Toba children, as casual shorts, shirt, catapults and clay bullets would be replaced by blazer, flannels, school tie and messy dip-in pens; where the security of a bedroom in an adobe house would be exchanged for a dormitory with nine other boys; where parental discipline would give place to housemasters and prefects; where screeching cicadas would be replaced by the eerie whistles of the *sereno* (nightwatchman). I remember vividly one year leaving weeks late, travelling the first few miles through deep flood water to a makeshift home on higher ground and seeing my mother prepare all my clothes for school in the open forest. Life was full of the unexpected!

The regular carter was Modesto Dagachalo'n, a traditional

Modesto Dagachalo'n, the carter

Toba who always wore a flowing native skirt rather than trousers and had his hair very long. He would sit up front on the four-wheeler next to my father. Modesto held and controlled the three mules from the cart with one hand and the whip in the other, although most commands were given by shouts. His brother Jacinto Chidiñi'n was the outrider, encouraging the mules forward and holding them back should they move too fast.

The cart journey to the railhead at Ingeniero Juárez was a 90 kilometre trek, usually taking a day and a half. There were recognised stopping places on the road where water would be available for the mules and hopefully some pasture, usually a waterhole covered with green weed. If there was no grass, branches of *algarrobo* or *chañar* would be cut to feed the mules. Prior to resuming the journey next day, they would be fitted with nosebags containing maize: the sound of mules' teeth grinding the dry sweet corn is one I remember with fond nostalgia.

Nights on the road were memorable. A large black mosquito net would be set up, firewood which was readily available was collected and a large fire lit. If mosquitoes were around, dry pads of cow dung were collected and lit, allowing the breeze to carry the acrid smoke across the area where we were camping, filling our eyes with tears but hopefully keeping the mosquitoes away.

The Winchester 22 and double-barrel shotgun were leant against a tree trunk. A three-legged pot was placed on the fire and boiled rice prepared and mixed with corned beef or sardines and eaten with hard biscuits. We all sat by the fire and grace was said before the meal, Modesto reverently removing his headscarf allowing his long hair to fall around his shoulders. We slept on the ground under a clear sky, its abundance of stars twinkling at us through the mosquito net.

Flitting fireflies dotted the dark to a chorus of hooting owls and barking foxes. While the mules and horses were tethered by the green weed-covered waterhole, foxes, probably attracted by the smell of food, would sometimes approach and gnaw through the leather lasso, inadvertently releasing one of the mules.

The journey would resume early after a breakfast of dried biscuits and *mate cocido* (hot sweet green tea). The mules would be harnessed and tied in and we were once more on our way, taking advantage of the cool early morning.

6
One horse town

BY LATE evening Modesto would be shouting his last "*Vamos…vamos!*", probably all the Spanish he knew, as he whipped the mules and Ingeniero Juárez finally came into sight, a real one horse town! It had a population of just on 2,000 with two main general stores, one owned by Manuel Vidal, a Spaniard, the other by Abraham Jaluf from Syria. They had followed the construction of the railway, undertaking business with the many employees, and now on its completion they remained in Juárez to supply the Bolivian and Paraguayan forces across the Pilcomayo.

The first building to come into view as the road straightened was the station, a solid brick structure on the south side of the town. Perversely Juárez has developed to the north, leaving the station on the 'wrong side of the track'. Close to the main station building is a huge warehouse, quite outsize for the town, but no doubt built with thoughts of housing provisions and perhaps armaments for the ongoing Chaco War.

With a cry of "Buenos Aires!" Modesto would pull in the reins and move the cart off the road into a shady spot not far from a carpenter's shop which at that time was the first home as you entered the town. The carpenter was a Bolivian called Enrique Torres. With the exception of the station, all the other buildings were precarious wooden structures hastily put together. The most presentable was the Civil Registry (where my parents married), a wooden prefab cast off by the railway constructors after the line was finished.

Once the mules had been unharnessed, removed from the shafts and the fire lit, the first visit was to Jaluf's store. He was a kind of 'agent' for the mission, collecting the mail and any other consignment that arrived by rail and supplying the mission store with its provisions. This general store provided the basics of flour, sugar, ground maize (corn), *yerba* and rice. The sugar came in sacks weighing 70 kilos, labelled 'Leach's Argentine Sugar Estates', while the salt arrived in large solid blocks similar to those provided for cattle and had to be broken up with hammers. Bottles of pure alcohol were openly displayed on the shelves, whilst coca leaves were hidden under the counter but sold freely by the gram.

Indians were employed to unload the goods trains and to load the carts and lorries. They were mostly coca-dependent and were recompensed at the end of the day with a handful of coca leaves, some soda bicarbonate and a bottle of alcohol. It was virtual slave labour. You still see notices for the sale of *'coca y bic'*, although it is illegal.

Jaluf, though a Syrian, was referred to as a *turco* (Turk), like all Arab immigrants. On one occasion he was driving his lorry along a muddy forest road with my father alongside when he suddenly broke into a chorus of "Stand up, stand up for Jesus"! My father's amazement was increased when he told him he had been brought up in a Christian village school in Syria. I am afraid, though, that it had little effect on his business ethics. The only word these *turcos* understood in Toba was *kachagaik*, meaning 'thief'—they must have heard it repeatedly.

I once asked one of these storekeepers to what he attributed his and his parents' material success, since they had arrived in the port of Buenos Aires with only the baskets they could carry, many of them illiterate and unable to spell or even pronounce their surnames in understandable Spanish. His reply was just one word—*aguante*—endurance, perseverance. Besides this *aguante,* they seem to have the ability to sniff out potential business opportunities. Whereas the Englishman's ethic is "the customer is always right" and if treated well will come again, the *turco's* would seem to be "get all you can by whatever means as the customer may not return"!

Today's train tomorrow

The timetable for the twice-weekly passenger train was related more to the day than the hour. The train usually passed through Juárez during the dark hours; the practice of the potential passenger was to enquire the time of arrival before setting off with luggage from home to the station. A bell was rung to announce the train's departure from the previous station, which guaranteed at least an hour before its arrival unless it ran into a cow and derailed.

The arrival of the train at whatever hour was a great social occasion. People waited on the platform alongside goats tied to the metal pillars, a label stuck to their rump with a glue made of flour and water. Their droppings lay all round the pillar. Pigs were placed in wooden cages and poisonous snakes being forwarded to the snake farm were in special containers. If the passenger train was the one following the previous day's cattle train, then many of the passengers would be the *chaqueño* cowboys following their cattle for sale in Embarcación. They would travel resplendent in polished boots, wide *bombacha* trousers with an embroidered handkerchief protruding from the back pocket, white embroidered shirts and broad-rimmed hats. Wine ran freely and conversations became animated, as did the singing. Those skilled as raconteurs would display their talents as they responded antiphonally in a monotone chant from one end of the carriage to the other, recounting anecdotes of the rough, rustic life they led with their horses, cattle and their women.

At the sound of the station bell, tickets would be sold—not before, in case the train failed to arrive! As I waited for my ticket, I always found it fascinating to watch a member of the station staff communicating in Morse and tapping out messages with dot-dot-dashes. The one-way phone system informing the names of the engine driver, fireman and guard also captivated me. I recall one occasion when a goods train was delayed because of a missing guard. The crisis was resolved when someone noticed he was in the local bar. The waster was hauled out and manhandled in his drunken stupor into the caboose and the train sent on its way!

When the train eventually arrived, manoeuvres and shunting took place, lanterns being swung to indicate to the driver when couplings had been completed. Depending on his expertise, these could cause great bumps rather like falling dominoes as the effect moved down along the line of carriages, a phenomenon particularly observable on a long goods train. The signalman would then climb the iron ladder and place oil lamps on the signals. Having gathered sufficient steam, the train with a shrill whistle-blast would pull out of Juárez, three goods vans at the front immediately behind the engine, then the second class carriages, followed by the first class, then the dining car and finally a sleeper.

Modesto, his mules and the four-wheeler would soon be making their way back to Misión El Toba, where my mother would be happy to know I would be afforded a good education, but sad that I wouldn't be home again for nine months. For me, the sadness of leaving for school was mitigated to an extent by the novelty of the train journey, although I remember that when we crossed with another train I was always jealous of those travelling in the direction of my home.

Alfred Leake (centre) with Colin Smith and Severiano Zanja on an exploratory visit to the Pilcomayo

Alfred riding through swampland in Paraguay

7
School years 1944-52

MY PARENTS' background and schooling did not give them the experience to prepare me for a British-style boarding school education; consequently, when in 1944 I went to school in Buenos Aires at the age of eight, I entered a strange new world for which I was ill-prepared. On the first day I recall asking after lunch where we would sleep for siesta and being told in no uncertain terms by one of my seniors that this was not part of the timetable! My lack of Spanish meant I spent two years in the Second Grade with a well remembered teacher called Angelica Hunter, whom I had the privilege of meeting again when I moved as bishop to Buenos Aires 45 years later.

I was regarded as different since I had come from a peculiar background of life amongst the Indians. I was quickly nicknamed Toba and alternatively Cebolla (Onion) which was the nearest translation the boys understood for Leake! School life was highly regimented and ruled by bells and gongs. Uniform was strictly observed: black shoes, grey socks, grey shorts, white shirt with school tie and a blue blazer with the school badge. Some still wore the school cap.

Discipline was harsh, with written impositions and regular beatings for misbehaviour, or being gated and not allowed out for an exeat. Impositions included copying out Chapter 3 of a geography text entitled *Southern Continents*. Written copies of this chapter had commercial value, and when in need of a few cents you would make copies for sale to those who had not made time to prepare their punishment. You could be ordered to write alternate words in blue and red ink, and since we still used dip-in pens this became an exercise in manual gymnastics. Failure to remember chemistry formulae resulted in having to write out lengthy copies of them, and in spite of my having to do this many times, the only one that remains with me is H_20!

During my first months I was proud of the novelty of being called by my surname and saying “Present, Sir”. The older boys were appointed prefects and exerted quite a bit of authority. They were even allowed to inflict corporal punishment and had fags to undertake menial tasks.

The model was the English public school system of the time, with school ‘houses’. I was allocated to Corinth, the other two being Athens and Sparta, names whose initials came cleverly together to form SAC which corresponded with the name of the school - St Alban’s College. It was very competitive. Yet I adapted to the new life and demands and now look back to school days, maybe not as happy ones but certainly with appreciation; it was a formative time.

Cricket and rugby were played in season. I was not a great sportsman, but during my last year played in the 1st XV. Soccer was frowned upon as a game played by the ‘naps’, street boys.

I remained as a boarder for the next nine years. The war in Europe was still raging and many boys who might have been sent to Britain for schooling remained in Buenos Aires. Many of them were the sons of families working for the British railways or other companies in Argentina and many others were from *estancias* (large farms) scattered across the Pampas and Patagonia. The majority of the boys came from English-

In the 1st XV at school

speaking homes and bore English surnames, and the English spoken was precise and correct, if at times archaic: we spoke of frocks instead of dresses, of ice chests instead of fridges. There was also a splash of 'Spanglish', with words like 'collation' meaning jumping the queue (from the Spanish *cola*) and 'inching' for being a nuisance (from the Argentine slang *hinchar*). Transliterations such as 'to molest' (from Spanish *molestar*, to disturb), and to 'pateate' the ball (from the Spanish *patear*, to kick), were often heard in conversations.

Painful memories

Marching formed a large part of Physical Training exercises and woe betide anyone who inadvertently finished on the wrong foot. There would be a shout of “Bricks…Bricks”, meaning that instead of one stamp by the squad halting all at once, boys had all halted at different times and with different feet like a load of tumbling bricks! The nearest culprit to the PT instructor would get a rap of knuckles on the head.

In all dormitories talking was prohibited after lights out. If any whispering was heard by the duty prefect on his rounds, the lights were immediately switched on and the fearful question “Who was talking?” uttered. If no one owned up, all the boys in the dormitory had to get out of bed, kneel down and the prefect would go round the lot with a slipper. In the midst of such harsh discipline, I can remember covering my head with my sheet and dreaming of my horses, my catapult and my Indian friends.

Public School on the Pampas

The public school system of education was, like the railways, a legacy of British influence in Argentina. The principal school, St George’s College, founded in 1898 by Canon Stevenson, was a remarkable boarding institution complete with chapel, rugby fields and swimming pool, and was represented on the Headmasters’ Conference.

St Alban’s College, where I studied, was founded in 1907 by the Revd George Henry Knight-Clarke, but did not enjoy such good amenities and had day-boys as well as boarders. The founders of both schools came to Argentina with other ecclesiastical responsibilities, but subsequently moved into the field of education. They were not church schools, but both had an established basic discipline of regular prayers and church attendance twice on Sundays.

St Alban's was less affluent, fees were not so high, and the school could not afford to contract many staff from Britain. Yet it was well served for many years by Charles Cohen, a highly qualified Cambridge graduate and a very able wicketkeeper. Charles came from a wealthy Christian family who had settled in Argentina. His mother and sister Faith had always shown great sympathy and kept open house for the missionaries who worked in the north of the country. Later I was to discover that Mrs Cohen had generously helped with my school fees.

Charles with his wife Margaret ran a Bible Study group known as Crusaders in their home every Sunday. No doubt many who attended did so as a legitimate means to get out of school and enjoy rich cakes at teatime, or to have access on the way to a radio at the service station to hear the football results. But others were certainly challenged as to their Christian commitment, amongst them Luis Palau who went on to become a world-famous evangelist. Charles Cohen was a kind of conscience for the school, and although his sense of discipline was severe and six of the best with a cricket bat was not uncommon, he was highly respected and his teaching was of the highest calibre.

Letters and dreams of home

Letters home had to be written every week. For the boarders time was given on Saturday afternoons for Letter Writing Rough Copies, in which you would write your letter, which was then corrected by the master on duty. This was then

Prefects at St Alban's College (I am in the middle)

copied out on school headed paper on Sunday morning before going to church. Besides the compulsory corrected letter, you were allowed to write further letters to parents and stick the envelope down during the week. My mother kept all my school letters and they in some way reflect, albeit in a stilted manner, my experiences, thoughts and inclinations during my school years. Meantime letters and replies from my parents were eagerly awaited and were read and re-read.

Bullies, punch-ups and inspections

Fights would break out between boys and they would quickly be surrounded by a group of spectators supporting one or the other. I remember being bullied and having my pocket money regularly taken every week by an older boy. Pocket money days on Wednesday and Saturday became times to be dreaded, but on one occasion I stood my ground and refused to hand it over. My assailant took me threateningly by the arm and a punch-up ensued, quickly drawing a crowd, many of whom shouted their support for me. In a moment of whirling arms and fists, mine hit him firmly on the nose, which started to bleed profusely, and I was declared the winner. From that day onwards I never had any more trouble.

8
Dreams and values

WHILST I lived in my 'other world' at school, my thoughts would often turn to my parents and two sisters in Misión El Toba. I was the eldest, with Cristina, named after a Toba Indian, next in line. She was sensitive, academically gifted and single-minded. From an early age she set her mind on becoming a doctor, an objective she achieved after her medical course at Leeds University, where she met and later married Dr Trevor Hunt.

Like me, she was born at Misión El Toba where Aunt Olive was still available to attend my mother. Her early playmates were the Toba girls and she became proficient in their language and customs, fetching wood from the forest and collecting the algarroba beans and the prickly pear that grew around our home.

We enjoyed this fruit, although collecting it from the tall cacti was not without pain. It was taken with a piece of cow's horn attached to a long pole; you had deftly to cover the fruit with the horn and twist. The fruit was then placed in a small string-net bag which you shook vigorously, making sure you weren't on the windward side to avoid being covered by the small, almost invisible, thorns. Inevitably after collecting the fruit we would find many of these thorns in our hands and bodies. We would eat the prickly pear as dessert at mealtimes or my mother would make jam.

Cristina followed me to Buenos Aires to undertake her education at Barker College, a girls' boarding school, which had a motto that would not be acceptable today for a girls' school: *Manners maketh Man*!

The Sunday Crusader class at Charlie Cohen's was a happy weekly meeting place for Cristina and me, and our paths also crossed when we attended Holy Trinity church. She excelled in sport and in her studies, passing her Overseas Cambridge Examinations. Like the other British schools, both Barker College and St Alban's College followed the Argentine Ministry of Education curriculum for primary education in Spanish, and the English curriculum led to the Overseas Cambridge School Certificate Examinations. Study was demanding in that we followed not only two curricula but also two languages. When Cristina had completed all that Barker College could offer her, she moved for a year to Quilmes High School where she served as a student teacher and completed further examinations.

Of the three of us, probably Dorothy became the most proficient in the Toba language and the most sensitive to the Indian culture. She established deep friendships with Modesto's daughters and the little daughter of one of her friends became her bridesmaid at her wedding to Philip Miller in Misión Chaqueña. Dorothy also followed Cristina to school at Barker College.

Foundational values

My time away at school was an impressionable period in my early life, and in spite of demands and strict discipline it is a time to which I look back with appreciation. Foundations were laid and values established. The secure love of my parents, their solid marriage and our happy family life left me in no doubt where I belonged. Boarding schools later became a kind of paid care centre for the children of wealthy divorced parents. In my own time at school, when a boy's parents separated it was spoken about in hushed tones. But when my son was at boarding school, he said that Rachel and I were out of the ordinary since a high percentage of his friends' parents were separated.

Boyish escapades

But there were escapades, and one in particular became much talked about. It occurred during one of the various political upheavals in Argentine history at the time of the campaign in support of Balbín and Frondizi of the Radical Party. Donald Sym-Smith, a fellow-prefect, and I were responsible for the España Annexe, and together with Donald Marshall, we decided that one night after lights out we would take the train into Plaza Constitución to participate in the political demonstration. We had to saw through a metal bar to have space to climb out of the upstairs window. It took a few nights to saw right through the bar and we would put the radio on loud enough to disguise the noise and hide the cut section of the bar by tying the cord from the shutter around it until we could carry on sawing the next night. Once the bar had been cut through, we could bend it outwards, affording ourselves space to climb out of the window.

But the political meeting turned violent, mounted police intervened, and one man was shot and fell down the stairs leading to the underground. The police with drawn swords galloped through the crowd dispersing it. Sym-Smith, Marshall and I made for the protection of the station, but when we arrived the main gates were closed. After a while they were reopened and the crowd surged into the main hall. We attempted to escape by going downstairs to the toilets but were confronted by police pointing pistols at us, and so we made for the platform. By this time our eyes were streaming from the tear gas and we held on to the rails that surrounded the buffers to avoid being trampled in the stampede.

In due course things calmed down and we were able to get the train back to Lomas de Zamora. On arrival we went to the Munich bar for a Quilmes beer and prepared for the re-entry into the annexe. This was more complicated than our exit as we had to climb a wall, move gingerly along a fragile corrugated iron roof, undo the cord to the shutter, bend the iron bar outwards, and pull ourselves back through the window.

In loco parentis

Mrs Doris Neve, wife of the Revd Arthur Neve who was the representative of the British and Foreign Bible Society, kindly acted as a kind of 'foster mother' while I was at school in Buenos Aires. They lived in Florida in the Northern Suburbs and had three daughters who attended Northlands School in Olivos; decades later this would be the suburb where Rachel and I would live for 12 years whilst I was Bishop of Argentina. I remember weekend visits and particularly recall an incident when they entertained British Naval personnel while their German neighbours entertained members of the crew of the *Graf Spee*. Hosts and visitors eyed each other through the hedge.

The Neves' grandson, Tim Curtis, who is the son of their

late daughter Irene and Tom Curtis, follows his grandparents in promoting knowledge and distribution of the Bible, having been involved for many years in the translation of the Scriptures into the language of the Enxet Indians in the Chaco area of Paraguay.

Choir, crucifer and Confirmation

Sundays were busy. Besides attending Crusaders in the afternoon at Charles Cohen's, we went to church at Holy Trinity twice, walking by twos in crocodile formation. Prior to leaving, we were each given 20 cents by the duty master to put in the collection. The church was close to the railway line and when the steam train thundered past it was impossible to hear anything else. It is said that when the church was originally built and administered by the British, there was a gap in the timetable on Sunday mornings when no trains passed for 20 minutes to give the vicar time to preach his sermon unhindered!

In due course, I became a member of the choir. We received a small imbursement for singing on Sundays and going to choir practice, and there was also the perk of singing at weddings. If the reception was held in the church hall, we were included and were expected to take sandwiches and cakes back to our dormitories to provide a midnight feast for the other boys.

I became crucifer and led the choir in procession. Many years later, I made a pastoral visitation to Holy Trinity in my capacity as bishop and recalled this practice as I entered now last in the procession. It placed a new slant on the text "The first shall be last"!

Church services were traditional, rigidly following the Book of Common Prayer. I do not remember any particular sermon or specific spiritual experience, but would certainly say that the formality and regularity of worship endued me with a sense of the majesty and transcendence of God. Both church services and evening prayers at school memorably impressed on my mind for all time words from collects and hymns. I was prepared for Confirmation by the Revd William Franklin and confirmed by Bishop Daniel Ivor Evans in 1951. My letters to my parents recall this event.

These formal celebrations of the Christian faith, as well as the more personalised experience of Bible studies at Charles Cohen's home, nurtured and maintained my faith during the years I was at school. Luis Palau, a school friend who was to become a well known evangelist, kindly observed: "I simply did not live for God during the rest of my school days at St Alban's College and my summers at home. I knew deep down that I belonged to Christ, but to me the pressure not to be considered a fool was too much. I stood by and let the other two or three Christians at St Alban's carry the ball for the Gospel. Henry Martin and David Leake were two of the other confessed Christians, and I always felt bad that I was hardly in their league as a witness. Leake, now a bishop in the Anglican Church, did not flaunt his faith. He never talked piously. He was just himself, and was admired and respected" (*The Luis Palau story,* p.61).

This is very kind of Luis Palau. I am happy with the comment and hope it was true!

9

Toba in Norfolk

THE AGREEMENT with the South American Missionary Society was that my parents were entitled to home leave every five years. But owing to the war it was impossible to make the journey and consequently an extended period of 10 years passed without a visit to grandparents and family in England.

The last time my parents had been on leave was in 1939, and then they only just managed to get back to Argentina before the outbreak of war. My father spent most of that leave as a student at the London College of Divinity. Although Bishop Weller had offered to ordain him in Argentina after an essay course, my father had insisted that he did not want to "enter the ministry by the back door". At that time there were those who were regarded as being in second-rate "Colonial Orders". My father was ordained Deacon by letters demissary on a cold day in Canterbury Cathedral by Archbishop Cosmo Gordon Lang.

After those 10 years in Argentina, in 1949 we travelled as a family to Britain for a period of extended leave. We sailed on the *Empire Deben* which I believe was a prize of war; it had been fitted out as a troop ship and there were still hammocks in some sections and the large number of us children had great times playing hide and seek. The passengers were allocated the officers' quarters.

In England we stayed with my mother's parents in a small cottage in the High Street of East Runton, next door to the garage and bicycle shop where my mother used to have her bike repaired as a girl!

In order not to lose the rhythm of studies, I was sent with my sisters to the village school, where I felt like a fish out of water. I had been used to half-day teaching in Spanish and the other half in English, while the English I spoke and heard in Buenos Aires was very different from that of North Norfolk. Being a day-boy was also different to being a boarder: there was less competitiveness, no houses and no monthly reports, and I found I had nothing in common with the other village children. My parents realised I was unhappy and arranged for me to move to Beeston Regis Hall School.

This school had recently moved from Walsingham. The Headmaster, Mr Tapping, and his wife were very understanding and I think were pleased to have someone 'a little bit out of the ordinary' to add to the spectrum of school life. I felt much more at home and understood the system. We played rugby and cricket. My Spanish pronunciation of the Latin verbs was highlighted by Mrs Tapping who commended me and would comment: "Boys, listen to Leake's pronunciation."

I was at the school for just two terms, yet it was a significant and memorable time and a further experience to add to those among the Tobas and the Anglo-Argentine life in Buenos Aires.

Return to Buenos Aires

Time in England passed quickly and we were soon on our way back to Argentina. I was a little despondent that I would have to go straight back to school and not be able first to go to the north to see my Toba friends and my horses!

Our return voyage to Buenos Aires was more upmarket

since we sailed on the Royal Mail Steamer *Andes*. Passenger air flights from the UK to Argentina were still in their infancy. The voyage gave us a wonderful 21 days' holiday and relaxation with lots of interest and entertainment. The ship called at Cherbourg, Vigo and Lisbon, Canary Islands, Rio de Janeiro and Santos, with opportunities for outings in each port.

The final part of the journey from Montevideo to Buenos Aires was the most irksome since Argentine immigration officials would board the ship and overnight examine and stamp all passports and other documentation. It was also noisy due to vibration as the 26,000-ton vessel scraped the bottom of the shallow River Plate. I always found the arrival at port fascinating as the pilot boat came out followed by the tugs, orders were shouted and lines thrown ashore, and finally the ship was tied up and the gangway put in place.

Argentine Customs were always a big unknown hurdle to face; in a country where bribery and corruption are rife, it was an unnerving experience. I remember one missionary defining bribery as paying someone to do something they should not do, in contrast to an incentive which was to pay someone as an encouragement to get them to do what they should do.

My father on his outward journey to the UK had taken a big oil tin full of honey and bought a large bunch of green bananas in Brazil, knowing that his family in England were still on rations.

He brought back bits and pieces of army surplus which he thought would be useful in the Chaco, including field telephones and metres of telephone wire, as well as a rubber dinghy to float down the Pilcomayo.

On arrival in Argentina, my parents returned to our home in the north and my sisters and I to our boarding schools in Buenos Aires. To have had the opportunity of travelling to the UK during my school days was a great novelty and I returned to school a kind of hero, especially as I arrived with English W.D. & H.O. Wills cigarette tins (empty, I hasten to add) and other novelties and mementoes from the ship.

My period in England meant I advanced in my English education, but lost a year with my Spanish grades. I had therefore to undertake my sixth grade as *Libre*, in other words, double up and do two grades at the same time. This meant a cycle ride out of school every day to Señorita María Gladys Uriona as my private teacher. In due course I went to Colegio No.1 near the main square in Lomas de Zamora to sit my exam. I was one of very few doing an exam, and in the course of it a teacher sidled up to my desk, looked to see how I was getting on and asked if she could be of any help. When I insisted I was doing fine, she moved on. As I emerged from the room, Señorita Uriona was waiting for me and reprimanded me for not getting the teacher—whom she had sent into the room—to help me! Anyway, with or without help, I managed to get through my sixth grade. The next three years were concentrated on working towards the Overseas School Certificate as set by the Cambridge University Examinations Board.

The rhythm of school and journeys home for holidays continued until 1952 when I completed my secondary education. During our last year my friends and I had to consider what work we would undertake. A relatively easy option was the Bank of London and South America (now Lloyds); with fluent English and Spanish there was usually a place for school leavers, and some of my friends went on to responsible posts there in later years. Another option was to go as a 'Second' to an *estancia*. This was an apprenticeship on a ranch with the eventual appointment as an administrator or foreman. Unlike today, few boys moved on to study in Argentine universities.

The option to work on an *estancia* appealed to me, but the immediate prospect of returning home on holiday was a strong pull. My father offered me the opportunity to work for a year on the mission station and be responsible for the store with the buying and selling of native crafts, as well as organising and documenting the branding of the Indians' horses and donkeys. Not surprisingly, I opted for my father's suggestion.

I awaited the results of my School Certificate examinations with trepidation, and remember to this day where I was when I opened the envelope. I had ridden to Juárez and collected the mail from Jaluf's store. Spotting amongst the letters one with the distinctive school badge on the envelope, I stuffed it into the saddlebags and only when I was well on the way home did I dismount and open it. Following the printed heading 'Overall Assessment' was one word written by the headmaster, Mr J.E. Vibart: 'Rejected'.

In those days you had to pass at least five subjects, including English Language. I had failed English Language.

10
Return to paradise

MY 'job description' back in Misión El Toba was simple but exciting as I would be doing all the things I enjoyed and be paid a small remuneration. I was to be responsible for the general store; the bell announced its opening twice a day, mid-morning and mid-afternoon. This was seen as an important part of the mission presence amongst the Indians as it afforded the opportunity to provide them with basic necessities at fair trade prices and also an outlet for their crafts which, in the Tobas' case, were woven materials. Besides the sale of flour, ground maize, sugar and *yerba*, there were dyes for the wool, pencils and exercise books. Printed patterned cloth was sold by the metre, plus fish hooks, gunpowder and lead shot as well as the empty cartridges to be made up, and also permanganate of potash for snakebite.

The Indians returning from the sugar plantations were paid in kind and would often arrive with superfluous personal and household items which were bought by the store and then resold, often to the Argentine settlers who were pleased with the opportunity to buy a hat, saucepan, bucket or spade. The small profit allowed us to buy medicines. These were the days before NGOs and other charities financed development and relief.

With no plastic bags or wrapping paper, flour and maize were wrapped in a headscarf or tucked in a skirt. I even witnessed a father taking his young son's trousers off, knotting the legs and putting sugar down one and *yerba* down the other! Merchandise was weighed on a pair of scales with two metal plates, between which were what I always thought looked like the heads and extended beaks of two storks. When these were even and just balanced in favour of the buyer, the correct weight had been given.

Supplies for the store came from Abraham Jaluf in Juárez, often by big, springless two-wheeler carts pulled by six mules, similar to the one that my father had originally arrived in, and taking three to four days to make the journey.

The alternative was Jaluf's lorry, whose arrival became the event of the month. Long before it arrived, the Indian children would hear the drone of the engine and the excited chorus of *"Camión! Camión!"* would be heard everywhere. For the last 200 metres of its journey it was surrounded by barking dogs and racing, cheering children, some of whom would cling on the tailboard for a ride, completely unaware of the danger. Its unloading became almost a theatrical comedy as men, in the midst of giggling women and jovial banter, volunteered to carry the heavy 70 kilo sacks into the store. My responsibility was to check that all sacks unloaded corresponded to the order list.

Horse branding and certificates

Unlike the Matacos, the Tobas were keen horsepeople and owned a good number of animals. The problem was that the Argentine settlers would often take their horses and brand them, leaving the Indians with no legal resources to make their claim of ownership. The mission therefore registered a brand with the relevant government office in the "Brands and Ear Marks" archive. The symbol initially chosen by the missionaries was the outline of the acorn (reminiscences of the

British oak!), but this was later changed as it bore similarity to one already registered. The new brand was a combination of the letters 'E' and 'G', the Spanish initials of the mission superintendent Henry Grubb. These letters were inverted making the symbol look like '63', and thus it was always described and became well recognised and respected.

Saturday, when many Tobas from outlying villages would ride to the central mission, was the regular day for branding. Rather like the day the lorry arrived with merchandise for the store, horse branding became a social event at which people would gather to watch the lassoing and the throwing of the horse. Once it was branded the owner was issued with a certificate of ownership, a highly prized piece of paper which provided a safeguard against theft. In the event of the animal being sold, the certificate had to be presented and the corresponding transfer certificate issued. The Indians valued this security, enjoying and attaching great importance to the bureaucracy, as they did with all documentation, such as licences, certificates and medical cards, all of which were originally rolled up and placed in a hollow piece of cane to keep safe and dry.

The three 'Rs'

Another area in which I became much involved was adult literacy, with a group of young men, my contemporaries, coming to me for a daily lesson. They were willing and desirous to learn, and many of them in later years became nursing orderlies or teachers, while others took minor political appointments in the provincial government department relating to Native Affairs, appointed and financed by the state.

Seeking to improve their Spanish was one of the key areas of interest.

My work enabled me to understand that expressing the Christian faith included a wide spectrum of activities and experiences. Safeguarding people's rights and ownership of land and animals, giving them a fair deal, seeking to provide them with tools to face the future, were all expressions of empowering the poor, what would today be called 'holistic ministry'. Many years later in Buenos Aires I was interviewed by a journalist from the principal daily *La Nación* and I mentioned that the Anglican Church had always seen its work among the Indians as a "holistic ministry". He misinterpreted the English expression and wrote in the paper about the ministry being "whole-stick", explaining that the missionaries were endeavouring to bring and stick all together—probably not far from the intention!

All good things…

The year working on the mission had been thoroughly enjoyable. I had undertaken jobs I delighted in, my time was spent with Indian friends from childhood days, there was time to ride, fish and hunt wild pheasant in the forest. I had, however, to recognise that this lifestyle could not continue open-ended, although it was my parents who rationalised the situation rather than myself.

I would have been content to continue as I was and remain 'native', building my own adobe house and living by the River Pilcomayo with some horses, cattle and a few goats, surrounded by the smells and noises of the forest. A lifestyle reflected by Yeats, the Irish lyricist:

"I will arise and go now, and go to Innisfree,
And a small cabin build there, of clay and wattle made:
Nine bean rows will I have there, a hive for the honey bee,
And live alone in the bee-loud glade".

But it was not to be ...

Carancho (vulture), Toba shaman

11

Goodbye to paradise

BY 1952 my parents, who were due for home leave, felt it was time for their children to have wider opportunities and broaden their friendships with a view to future relationships. Whereas my sister Cristina kept her sights set on becoming a medical doctor, I had no clear idea of what the future held. I was turning my back on a life amongst the Indians in the forests of Northern Argentina, nine years at boarding school in Buenos Aires, and the year as mission storeman, so the uncertainty of moving to England was a prospect as daunting as it was exciting.

As a family we settled in my late grandparents' fisherman's cottage known as 'The Anchorage' by the village green in East Runton, the same cottage where my father was born and from where he left to go to Argentina in 1926.

I was given the opportunity to be a farm labourer in the village of Gresham, owned by Major William Batt, who was the Deputy Lieutenant of the County of Norfolk as well as being the chairman of the South American Missionary Society. Major Batt was a formidable figure with a distinguished military moustache. In his younger days he had had a dramatic Christian conversion and was now a well known layman in the Church Assembly of the Church of England, as well as a renowned evangelist undertaking effective and influential Christian work amongst undergraduates.

I cycled from East Runton to Gresham every day, leaving the cottage at 6.30, my first objective being to stay on my bike to the top of Davey Hill, and with the three-wheel gear I often managed it. I could tell if I was late by the points on the road where I met other labourers also cycling to work.

Every morning the labourers would meet for 'orders'. Mr Palmer would stand in the farmyard waving his walking stick and we would be allocated our tasks for the day. Despite the contrast with the hot forests of Northern Argentina and the Toba Indians, I enjoyed this new development, relating to Norfolk labourers and endeavouring to understand 'broad Norfolk'. At first I would mistakenly go and sit in the 'shed' for breakfast instead of the 'shade'. It also took a while to differentiate between a 'horse' and a 'house' and between 'boots' and 'boats'.

When it came to piecework hoeing sugar beet, the task was undertaken with professionalism and speed, whilst I have to confess that other duties were rather stretched out. I was allocated work that did not require too much expertise, like mucking out the pig sheds, collecting potatoes off the field in a horse-drawn tumbrel, and setting up the sheaves in stokes as the binder went cutting the corn. The shiny twisted metal fingers which tied the twine in a neat knot in the middle of every sheaf before it was smartly flicked out on to the ground merited special admiration for the inventor who patented the machine.

In the days before my back became a problem I had to load sacks of corn from the barns on lorries. I particularly enjoyed harvest time when I was allocated to a Massey-Harris Combine Harvester as the sacker. Before I gained sufficient expertise, my arms, hands and fingers suffered continual deep scratches from the four nails on which I had to hook the sacks. One outlet was opened and the sack filled by pouring corn. I would work the sack with my knees as it filled in order to even out the corn, and once full deftly close the flow and open the other outlet to fill the next bag which was already in place. Twine cut in lengths was ready to tie the mouth of the sack. The sack then went down the chute behind the harvester, and once there were three full sacks ready on the chute they were dropped off across the field to be collected by a lorry. It was a dirty job, and when the wind was blowing in the wrong direction I was covered in dust and awns scratching my neck and body.

I particularly remember as the combine harvester went around the field in ever smaller circles, as did the binder cutting the sheaves, the gamekeepers would move in with their guns to take shots at the rabbits as they ran from the diminishing shelter.

It was a work experience very different from Argentina, but interesting, exciting and good to be in the open countryside with farm machinery and a horse, and immersing myself in Norfolk culture.

Following sister back to school

Cristina began a course in the Science Department at Norwich City College before going to Leeds University, from where she qualified as a doctor. For my part, having failed my Overseas School Certificate I needed to get some basic qualifications, so, motivated by my sister, I decided also to apply for a place at the City College. I entered the Commerce Department and was noted down for five or six basic GCE subjects, including Spanish, which I took at Advanced Level. This was certainly no great achievement, but at least added one subject to the list!

The college was served by Olive Browning, a particularly gifted lecturer in history whose ability at enthusing her students was such that, to my surprise, I was awarded a top grade in History at O-level. Prior to this achievement, however, I made little progress and my report describes me as being "more interested in socialising than in studies".

The change in my academic fortunes came in a strange way. For reasons I cannot now recall, I was sitting in Norwich Reference Library glancing through the Church of England Year Book and looking at details and qualifications required for ordination. This 'chance' perusal led me to write to what was known in those days as CACTM (Central Advisory Council of Training for the Ministry), the body responsible for informing and selecting ordination candidates. I received a helpful reply encouraging me to continue in my studies at the City College and to contact the bishop of the diocese.

So I got in touch with Bishop Percy Mark Herbert and an interview was arranged. The bishop was an impressive and imposing character, the picture of the prelate in his smartly buttoned black gaiters. He must have been one of the last 'prince bishops'. I shall never forget seeing him at Norwich Thorpe station alighting from the London train. As he walked across the main hall all the railway staff tipped their caps in respect. His letters were the epitome of brevity, two or three lines at most.

Our time in North Norfolk coincided with the Revd Daniel

Dick being Vicar of Cromer. We attended Cromer Church and so I approached him with my thoughts of ordination and a possible future reference. Sadly, he was not too encouraging, being more interested in his pigs and goats. He made it clear that if he had his time over again he would be a naturalist rather than a vicar! In spite of this, I have never heard such sensitive and consistently good sermons preached Sunday by Sunday. As his recognition and contribution to my possible future vocation, he would ask me to read the lessons in church. He gave me no warning as to what they would be, simply pushing a piece of paper into my hand with the details as he passed in the procession. He was not sparing in his comments if I read badly or made a mistake. One Sunday the word 'controversy' appeared twice in the lesson. Unsure how to pronounce it, I thought the best solution was to pronounce it differently each time so at least I could be half right or only half wrong!

Cromer Church and North Norfolk were so different from Northern Argentina and the Indian churches and congregations by the River Pilcomayo. But I was happy with a sense of fulfilment as I continued at Norwich City College and spent my vacations working on the farm in Gresham.

12

Road to the cloth

ONCE I had set my mind on the ordained ministry as my calling and objective, my studies at the City College gained extra motivation which led to improved exam results. I cannot say that my inclination to the ministry or my Christian faith itself were the result of any Damascus Road spiritual experience. In fact, I think I'm a disappointment to some Christians who hope for a story of some dramatic experience to which one can put time and place! Equally, there have been those who said of my vocation: "Oh, I suppose you just followed your father's footsteps". To which I reply: "That could be a reason for not wanting to be ordained!"

I think it was the practicality of the Christian faith that made greatest sense to me. There is undoubtedly wickedness in the world, but at the same time much goodness. When you fail to fulfil or attain to certain standards or deliberately share in underhand dealings or behaviour, you feel bad. When you refuse to share in a demeaning action and strive to meet higher ideals, you feel better. Certainly from an early age I was conscious of right and wrong.

I had seen many Toba Indians who had experienced change from a real fear of evil spirits and its consequences, now confessing that they could sleep at night. This had made a deep impression on me, as did the rejection of long-practised cultural traditions such as killing one child when twins were born or burying the terminally ill before death. Reflecting on these matters later in life led me to appreciate the sensitivity with which the Christian message had been shared with them, since they retained many of their other traditional customs. The criticism often levelled at Christian missions by social anthropologists—that they eradicated all traditional culture—is unwarranted.

I gained sufficient GCEs for eventual acceptance at a theological college and also cleared my mind of the disastrous results which had haunted me since the day I opened the envelope containing my report with its chilling verdict, 'Rejected'.

Dual nationality and military service

I am an Argentine by birth and British by descent. Argentina only recognises one nationality, although latterly they have turned a blind eye to those with dual nationality and two passports. Whilst in England, I was called up by the British Army, but applied for deferment as I was a full-time student. My application was granted as compulsory conscription in Britain was coming to an end and I think the authorities were happy to have fewer conscripts. At the same time that this British deferment was running, I was applying for the same from the Argentine Army. A limited deferment was granted as I was a student, and in due course when I became a seminarian I became eligible for exemption as all theological students and ministers of all religions are exempt, providing they remain in religious orders until the age of 37. I applied under this clause and was granted exemption, this being stamped and sealed in my *Libreta de Enrolamiento* through the Argentine Embassy.

My application to undertake theological studies with a view

to ordination was accepted on condition that I first completed military service, this being considered a good and valuable experience. It would have been utterly impossible for the Church of England authorities to understand that it was a non-starter to suggest to the Argentine Army that I needed a deferment in order to serve in the British Army! However, conscription was abolished in Britain and so although initially I was called up by both Britain and Argentina, in the end I served with neither!

With the matter of military service cleared, I made my formal application to CACTM to attend a Selection Board. This was arranged and I set in motion a few other steps which I hoped would help make my CV more acceptable. I joined the Toc H in Cromer, a group of men much older than me, mostly ones who had served in the Forces and been involved with Tubby Clayton and Talbot House. I was given a warm welcome and the activities and social concerns in which they were involved appealed to me. I also joined the local United Nations Association and was sent as delegate to the Annual Conference in Buxton, which I found interesting and appealed to my concern for world needs. In addition, I taught in the Sunday school in Cromer.

I enjoyed the Selection Conference where there were about twenty candidates, though I found the five days spent with some six interviewers challenging. Each interviewer was looking at some specific area of life experience, and during the five days an interview was held with each one within a timetable of prayer and devotions. At the end of the conference, the candidates left and the selectors evaluated them before opening their letters of reference. It was stressed during the conference that the purpose was not to think in terms of being accepted or rejected; rather it was a way of finding out God's will and purpose for our lives.

In due course I received a letter from CACTM telling me I had been accepted for training. The London College of Divinity attracted me because it was where my father had undertaken two terms of study in 1939; it had also been placed on the map of theological training through the influence of the Principal, Dr Donald Coggan, later to become Archbishop of Canterbury. An interview was arranged and I visited the college which at that time was temporarily installed in Ford Manor in Lingfield, having had its buildings in Highbury bombed during the war.

I do not recall details of my interview, but vividly remember dinner in hall! Those were still days of great formality: students wore academic gowns and rose from their benches at the long tables as the staff entered and grace was said. This was the setting and community I hoped soon to join. I was reminded of days at St Alban's College in Buenos Aires, with portraits of former principals and eminent former students gracing the walls, as well as the annual group photographs. Boarding school and regimented life had its appeal, and I decided I would be happy to spend a few years in this type of environment. The knowledge that I had decided on my life's work and passed the first hurdle of the Selection Conference was a sign that I must be moving in line with God's purpose for my life, and this gave me a sense of tranquillity and purpose. After my interviews I returned to

Student days at the London College of Divinity: I am in the middle row, fourth from the left

Norfolk where my mother kept home and a base for us whilst my father continued his work in Northern Argentina. During his time on his own with the Tobas he was seriously ill and cared for by Modesto's wife Jenague. Only later were we to discover just how ill he had been.

I received a letter from the vice-principal informing me I had been accepted as a student. Those were the days when grants were more readily available and I was fortunate to get one from the Local Education Authority in Norfolk to cover my three-year course to become an Associate of the London College of Divinity (ALCD). This, plus the opportunities to work on the farm in Gresham and at the Post Office at

Christmas, was sufficient to cover my financial needs. My sisters continued their studies and my mother, to help cover housekeeping costs, took a part-time job at the counter in the local baker's shop.

I looked forward to theological college. No suggestion was made at the time that I should first undertake a degree at university, something I have always regretted. My age and qualifications fitted me for the three-year diploma course at LCD, so I probably took the line of least resistance.

The college, which had a clear evangelical tradition, was, under Dr Coggan's guidance, broad-based in its theological outlook and had a good mix of students undertaking full University of London Bachelor in Theology degrees with other mature students doing the essay course. I found myself in the happy medium, the course being comprehensive and academically demanding. There was a mix of study and practical experience through hospital visiting and Sunday services, as well as visiting and taking services in an Epileptic Colony, as it was then called. These visits were particularly poignant since all those living in the colony suffered from some form of epilepsy, including young children with infrequent attacks and older people who wore a style of crash helmet to protect themselves when frequently falling.

Life was on a rather monastic style with Morning and Evening Prayer or Holy Communion every day, followed by private prayer and devotions. I would use this time to walk behind the college through a small wooded area. I felt a real closeness to God and prayer became very meaningful. Early in my first term we had tests in Bible knowledge and I remember being commended for my knowledge of Paul's missionary journeys, something I'd retained from school days in Argentina.

The main building at Ford Manor was full and a cottage had been rented in the village of Dormansland. I lived there with Charles May, Derek Head and John Watson. John had a small car in which we drove to the college; I regret it never occurred to me to offer to share the cost of petrol! John was to become a firm friend who served as best man at my wedding.

I must have talked *ad nauseam* about my life and experiences in Argentina, particularly in the Chaco amongst the Indians, and this was one day put to the test. Fred Crabb, the vice-principal, was appointed Principal of Emmanuel College, Saskatoon, and later as the Bishop of Cariboo in Canada. A special farewell was arranged on a theme related to Canada and to cowboys and Indians.

Derek Sawyer, a colourful character of an Anglo-Catholic persuasion and a good musician who later had a high-profile ministry in the United Kingdom, the Diocese of Mauritius and St Kitts in the West Indies, was keen on riding and borrowed a horse from the local publican. He was to be the Indian and dressed in his swimming trunks, had feathers in his hair and carried a bow and arrows. I was to be the cowboy with a large hat, tartan shirt and jeans. We secretly took the horse away from the college buildings to the bottom of the green, from where we planned to gallop to the ceremony to greet Fred Crabb, who was to be presented with a mitre complete with Davy Crockett tail.

Derek handed me the bow and arrows and mounted the

horse bareback. I tried to get on Indian fashion, using his outstretched leg and foot as stirrup, but inadvertently poked the arrow into the horse's rump. The animal jumped, depositing us on the ground, and then galloped towards the astonished guests. I understand the story is still recalled at college reunions 40 years later. From then on I talked less about my Argentine experiences.

13

Curate's egg

LIFE at college completed its course and I looked to final exams, then to ordination and a parish in which to serve my curacy. The presentation of diplomas and hoods was a memorable occasion, and I marvelled at the way I had come since childhood days running barefoot with my Indian friends in the Chaco.

My inclination was to serve in some needy parish in the north where the vicar was stressed and overworked; a generous sentiment, but I was given some opportune and wise advice that it would be better to serve my first curacy in a parish where things were on the move, with plenty of activity and a good vicar under whom I could train.

As it happened, things were taken out of my hands. I was contacted by the Revd John Downward, the vicar of Watford. John had always taken an interest in world mission and particularly in South America after hearing a talk by the great pioneer missionary Wilfrid Barbrooke Grubb at his Christian Union at Dulwich College. He was on the committee of the South American Missionary Society and from that source must have heard of my impending ordination and my links with Argentina.

John told me that plans had not worked out for him to serve as an overseas missionary, so he felt the next best thing would be to train an assistant who had strong connections with the church overseas and particularly in South America.

During my interview, John seemed keen to have me and presented a positive picture of the parish. He assured me the parish had no problems, which raised a smile from the wardens. He asked me what I expected of my vicar, and all I answered was "that he remain in the parish at least three years after I arrive". John briskly rubbed his hands together as was his custom, and made it clear he had no intention of leaving in that time.

St Mary's is the parish church of Watford, located in the middle of the shopping district just off the High Street. The church was set in the old graveyard known as the Garden of Rest, and the complex of vicarage, parish hall and an impressive historic building known as the Free School, together with a row of small, picturesque almshouses, formed a quiet precinct.

The only negative aspect was that the abattoir was not far away. On one occasion the steers escaped and ran amok, with some becoming impaled on the iron railings. The abattoir has since been moved.

The church had large congregations and former vicars had established a high standard of preaching ministry. Besides the vicar there was the first assistant curate, who had the title of Lecturer and historically had the responsibility of regularly giving a Christian lecture in the Market Place. There was also a second curate, a Church Army Sister, and a non-stipendiary priest, supported by no less than 50 voluntary workers leading the Scouts, Guides and Brownies, as well as the Covenanter leaders and Sunday school teachers, youth leaders and those caring for senior citizens, a group known as the Band of Cheer.

I felt privileged to be considered for the post of Assistant

Curate. I later met John's wife, Audrey, who was known to all as Mrs D and she fully complemented her husband. She was very practical, a great organizer, and had her two feet on the ground; I think she enjoyed regimented life and cut an impressive figure in her County Commissioner's Guide uniform. The vicarage was a model of orderliness and times were strictly adhered to. I must confess I had a slight feeling of nervousness in her presence, but I managed on my last visit to her in her retirement home in Sidmouth to call her Audrey instead of Mrs D! Both she and John left their mark on my ministerial life and my curacy of four years with them in Watford is one of the foundation stones of my future ministry, particularly when in later years I had to take responsibilities in Buenos Aires.

St Alban again

I was delighted to accept the invitation of John and the wardens to become the curate at St Mary's. I had interviews with the Bishop of St Albans, who was happy to accept me as a candidate for ordination and designated the Revd Canon Gordon Ireson to be my tutor and the person responsible for my post-ordination studies.

The date for my ordination was fixed for 21 September 1959 at the Abbey Church and Cathedral of St Albans. It was a happy coincidence that both my old school and the cathedral in which I was to be ordained were dedicated to the first British martyr.

During my pre-ordination retreat I felt that the steps I was taking were clearly set and timed by God: my clear sense of calling in the Reference Room at Norwich Public Library, passing the necessary exams to enter theological college, gaining a place at the London College of Divinity, and now the unexpected invitation to serve my curacy in Watford. I was like a ship moving into uncharted waters, but confident that the Captain on the bridge had his hand on the wheel.

I well remember the walk from the Diocesan Retreat House, Verulam House, to the Abbey. I felt happy but rather self-conscious in my clerical collar, cassock and surplice over my arm. The white stole in which I was to be ordained had been given to me by the Revd Alfred Tompkins, missionary colleague of my father in Northern Argentina and later vicar of All Saints, Quilmes, in the Province of Buenos Aires. He had inherited a set of stoles from the Revd George Henry Knight-Clarke, founder of the school I had attended in Argentina, and Alfred Tompkins felt it was appropriate that as an old boy of the school I should have them. On my retirement as Bishop of Argentina, I bequeathed them back to my old school.

My ordination as deacon was a memorable occasion. I was designated to be chalice-bearer at the Eucharist, with the celebrant the Rt Revd Michael Gresford Jones, Bishop of St Albans. I later came to know the bishop as a formidable figure and a man of deep spirituality; whenever he was walking in procession he would recite portions of John's Gospel to keep his mind concentrated on the service and occasion in hand. His first question before an interview in his study was: "And how is your prayer life?" I must confess that each time I was to see him I would make sure that for at least a fortnight beforehand I was praying in a disciplined way so as to be able to give a truthful answer!

The events of my ordination in St Albans Abbey have remained clear in my mind, and the year 1959 has always been a reference point or watershed, just like 1944 when I first went to boarding school in Buenos Aires. I returned to Watford to commence my ordained ministry in the Anglican Church, little knowing at the time all the exciting and fulfilling experiences it would afford.

Bad Aim

I was ordained at a time when the Church of England exerted a presence and influence that it perhaps does not have today. I remember my first Diocesan Synod, for which all 200 clergy had been summoned to St Albans. The city was certainly aware of the church's presence as cassocked figures walked around; a lasting record, the large group photograph, hangs in the studies of my contemporaries.

I enjoyed my curacy and in John Downward I had a good trainer who was demanding and generous. I was allocated to preach once a month and during the preceding week I had an interview in his study during which I had to read my script. As I preached, I knew he was sitting just behind me in his stall writing notes and comments, and as soon as I was back in the vestry he would go through his list. I remember one occasion when through nervousness I made excessive use of the word "situation". I was banned from using it for the next four sermons!

I once preached a sermon based on the book *Le Milieu Divin* by Teilhard de Chardin, whose writings were much in vogue at that time. I had obviously not fully understood Chardin's thesis, but had tried to digest and regurgitate some of his material. John's comment was: "Do not think that because you shot over people's heads you have superior ammunition. It shows you have very bad aim!"

In spite of his helpful criticisms, he was kind enough one Lent to give me the responsibility for preaching an entire series at the Lunch Hour services. His middle daughter, Rosemary, once asked her father, "Who's preaching on Sunday?" On hearing it was the curate, her counsel to me was, "Just five minutes and a joke." This comment has remained with me to this day, and whilst not to be taken literally, is a good challenge. If you can make people laugh they're likely to listen to you. Rosemary was later to marry Rachel's brother David.

My curacy days preceded the era of 'political correctness', investigations by the CRB did not exist, and information was more openly shared. Every Friday we visited the Peace Memorial Hospital where the matron would give us a pile of cards with the names of all newly admitted patients, their address and their religious allegiance. Those who declared themselves atheists were usually more interesting than those who just filled in 'C of E'. One man stated he was an atheist because his flat in the High Street was on a level with the church bells in the tower and he couldn't stand the noise on practice day and Sundays!

Registers had to be filled in clearly with black ink. John threatened that if a marriage certificate were inadvertently not signed in the vestry, the curate would have to find out where the couple had gone for honeymoon, follow them up, and get them to sign, as until then they were not legally married!

In those days the vicar was still regarded as the parson and the 'person' of the parish. John made it clear that he was spiritually responsible for the pastoral care of those in the parish and therefore would try to visit each home. After specific visits for baptisms, funerals or other pastoral needs had been covered, there was an ongoing plan to visit house to house, something I found nerve-racking, never knowing what response I'd get.

Industrial Chaplaincies were very much in the forefront of the Church's concern and a directive came from the bishop that each parish should make a survey of factories and industries and visit them. I was delegated to Benskin's Brewery. My first visit was quite frightening. Dressed in my charcoal grey suit and clerical collar, I contacted the Personnel Officer who kindly took me round, or rather from top to bottom, from the point where the hops came in right down to where barrels and bottles were loaded on to the lorries. The noise was tremendous; it was difficult to maintain a conversation, especially in the bottling area, nor could the workers just stop and have a chat with me.

I don't know if I did much good, but the experience certainly benefited me. There were spin-offs when a worker had an accident or a barrel squashed someone's toe and they had to go into hospital. They were pleased to be visited and I felt I had a point of contact and topic, often having met them in their workplace.

Most curates were not provided with a car, and the regular

means of getting around was a bicycle. This meant people saw the clergy 'on the job'. One occasion I was helping an elderly lady care for her ailing husband, and she needed a commode. I managed to locate one and took it rather precariously to her house on my bike. I expect any who saw me must have wondered if I was taking precautions in case I was caught with a stomach upset!

In such a parish every week had its funerals. The local funeral director undertook each occasion with much pomp, while the pallbearers and drivers had a particular sense of humour which I came to realise was a defence mechanism as they faced the reality of death every day. One in particular was a practical joker; on one occasion at the crematorium he was standing on the side of the coffin away from the mourners, so could not be seen. When I looked up from my Prayer Book to start the service, he had removed the light, round, artificial, metal handle on the coffin and hung it as though it were a nose-ring. It was all I could do to remain calm and composed; it was obviously a regular prank played on new curates.

The most tragic funeral was that of one of the Boy Scouts from the church group whose bicycle skidded one icy evening on his way to the Parish Hall and he fell under a lorry. John Downward designated me to officiate at the service. I found it difficult to get through without crying myself, and the whole congregation was moved as the pallbearers turned at the end to carry the coffin out with the Scouts' flag draped over it visible to all, the motto 'Be Prepared' sending a clear message.

The local crematorium in Garston became a place I regularly

visited. Ministry there required special adaptation as funerals were often of folk with no connection to the church and I faced the bereaved whom I had never met until the service itself. When it was the turn of our parish, I could be on duty a full day and have four or five funerals, one after the other. One day, in a forgetful moment, I asked someone at the door, "Are you waiting for the four o'clock one?" as though they were in line to see the dentist.

The different buttons you had to press for the music, the lowering of the coffin and the closing of the curtain, needed special care and concentration. I once pressed the button closing the curtain before time to the great distress of the widow who had been tearful and looking down. When she raised her eyes, she discovered her loved one had been for ever separated from her. It was literally 'curtains'. On another occasion, I erred over the alternatives "brother" and "sister" in the liturgy, and someone in an audible whisper corrected me with "brother!"

One of my first funerals was a tragic suicide, though I did not know this at the time. The traditional Prayer Book rubric establishes that such cases are not to be buried in consecrated ground nor, I believe, have an official Christian service. My feeling is that such tragic mental disturbance leading to suicide may well be no more the person's fault than any other psychological disturbance or physical illness. I took the service in the normal manner, believing the mourners needed more consolation and pastoral support in such circumstances.

The parish had a fairly large quota of weddings, with sometimes as many as four on a Saturday afternoon. John

Downward's advice was to have the West Indian couples at the end since they habitually arrived late. One bride was so late that I jokingly said to the chief bridesmaid: "You know, if the bride doesn't arrive, you have to take her place." She took me seriously and was momentarily petrified.

One time I was warned by the vicar that when I said, "If any of you know any cause or just impediment why these persons may not be joined together in Holy Matrimony, speak now or for ever hold your peace", the bride's mother might object. So I recited the words rather hurriedly, giving no time for interruption. There was no valid reason for any queries, the mother never uttered a word, and the service carried on smoothly.

Funerals, weddings and baptisms all required home visits, preparation classes and interviews. All served to immerse me in people's problems and hopes, doubts and uncertainties, and were opportunities for sharing at sensitive and impressionable moments in life the realities of the Christian faith, of God's love and concern for people, seeking to draw them into a relationship with Jesus Christ and hopefully into the family of the church.

The young curate was also expected to have some expertise with young people, so the Youth Fellowship was another of my responsibilities. Most young people at St Mary's were from Watford Grammar School and thus were an intellectually active and stimulating group. Among outings arranged were visits to the Proms, the public gallery of the Old Bailey, and an annual pilgrimage to St Albans Abbey at Easter. Many of the young people went on to assume positions of responsibility in music and education, one of them, Andrew Davis, becoming famous as conductor of the BBC Symphony Orchestra and being knighted for his services to music.

14
Rachel

JOHN Downward had strongly suggested that the timing of my engagement to Rachel Yarham should be before I came to the parish, a suggestion I was more than happy to go along with.

I had met Rachel whilst living in East Runton. Her parents were committed to Cromer parish where her father was for many years churchwarden, while her mother had a deep concern for missions. My parents and Rachel's met when her mother offered to become the local church secretary for SAMS. They shared information, ideas and resources on how to make mission in South America better known in the community.

Rachel accompanied her parents one evening when my father was giving an illustrated talk and I was projecting the slides for him. Rachel recalls this event as the first time she noticed me, and felt sorry for me since I continually put the slides in upside down or the wrong way round. Subsequent experience taught me there are eight ways of placing a slide in the projector and only one is right!

Rachel and I corresponded frequently whilst I was at theological college, but I found talk about girlfriends, fiancés and wives rather embarrassing since most students spoke of theirs as nurses, secretaries or belonging to some other profession and I had to admit that Rachel was still at school! Five years' difference seemed a lot when she was only 16 and I was 21. Nowadays, if I show some reluctance in extending a walk or am happy to sit and watch TV instead of doing some work at home, Rachel says: "Oh, I must remember you're five years older than me!"

We were formally engaged at the vicarage in Guist where my father had been appointed as rector in 1957 after retiring from Argentina. Guist was a small Norfolk village, the home of Sir Thomas Cook, grandson of the founder of the travel agent's, who lived with his family at the hall in Sennowe Park. My parents established a pleasant home in Guist, which had a large comfortable vicarage with an extensive garden and orchard. They settled well in the village, just as they had in the Chaco, and became part of the community. Being Norfolk-born they were accepted and understood the local people.

My father was also responsible for the church in the village of Twyford. Nowadays benefices in Norfolk are made up of five to 10 churches under the responsibility of a priest-in-charge, and if they are fortunate have some retired clergy to assist.

With just over a year to go before my curacy was due to be completed, Rachel and I fixed the date for our wedding. Rachel, now a nurse at Addenbrooke's Hospital in Cambridge, had visited Watford and so had an idea of where her first home after marriage would be, as well as some idea of what being wife to a curate might imply. We knew my senior colleague, Alan Rawe, was looking for a parish and would be departing soon, leaving a house which would become our first home.

Rachel and I were married in Cromer Parish Church on 30 December 1961. It was a memorable service on a very cold and rainy day, conducted by the vicar, the Revd Charles Searle-Barnes. My father took part and John Downward preached, making reference to his beloved Devon as he likened this new juncture in our lives to the Rivers Exe and Wye which flowed for a time almost parallel; then the Wye joins the Exe, takes its name and the two flow on as one in a deeper and wider course. I've often tried to use this anecdote in wedding sermons and to draw parallels between the rivers Pilcomayo and Bermejo, more familiar to me than the rivers of Devon, but have never quite managed it!

Rachel's bridesmaids were my sisters Cristina and Dorothy and her childhood friend Liz Ollis (*née* Bird). John Watson, my friend from theological college days, was best man, and filled the role admirably. In his speech he reminded Rachel not to wear the trousers as Moss Bros needed them back! We flew to Malaga for our honeymoon and returned to Watford to commence our ministry together.

Our first home was a semi-detached house, five minutes' walk from church. The top flat was occupied by the Church Army sister. I was continuing into my fourth year as curate and Rachel had just left her nursing after completing her State Registration. It was a big change for her to marry, leave a community of friends and a demanding job at Addenbrooke's, and move to Watford.

We worked together mainly amongst the young people, often arranging evenings in our home. My vicar delegated the representation for Inter-Church Aid (Christian Aid) to us and we spent time making this work known, also being responsible for the Flag Day and organising the collection of

On our wedding day

funds. I'm sure this involvement kept our minds focused on world needs. Rachel since childhood was drawn to the needs of leprosy work in Africa, my early life and experiences in the Argentine Chaco were never far from my thoughts, so we felt that some day we would serve in the church overseas. With this in mind, we made a point of not settling down too comfortably and buying furniture—I had been told that once you buy furniture it's difficult to move on!

15

Argentina back in focus

DURING our time in Watford it started to become clearer that we should work in Argentina. In my case it was confirmed through a series of practical realities. It would be too much to call the experience a vision or some supernatural revelation, but rather an evaluation of the practical gifts and circumstances of birth and early childhood which I felt pointed me in that direction. I imagined seeing the large collection plate on which the offerings were received in church, but the move was reversed. I felt I was being presented with the plate and on it were the gifts that God had given me.

On the plate was my *Libreta de Enrolamiento*, the identity document that every male Argentine citizen has to obtain at the age of 18, in which all details of military service or exemptions are recorded, as well as obligatory voting in elections. I also recognised a certificate for proficiency in Spanish and one for knowledge of Toba, as well as one accrediting knowledge and experience of life in Northern Argentina. All these practical and natural gifts were of no use in Watford and I felt they were a clear pointer that my future lay back in Argentina. Rachel's nursing experience and her inclination to service overseas were a further confirmation that this was the way God was guiding us, and so we set in motion the first steps towards Argentina.

We shared our vision and hopes with John Downward, who suggested we contact the South American Missionary Society.

An interview was arranged with the committee, and after an

initial uncertain reaction on their part we were invited to a second interview.

Their doubts were related to my broader sympathies in the expression of churchmanship. I said I was quite happy and at home with the use of a stole and taking eastward position at the Holy Communion, a stance some committee members found unacceptable! Our second interview satisfied them I was no ‘crypto-Roman Catholic’. Such subtle ecclesiastical inclinations and differences would be meaningless to most people today, but they were real issues at the time.

So we were accepted as candidates and began the countdown to South America.

Our first child, Andrew, was born at home during the very cold winter of 1962 and Rachel’s mother travelled from Cromer to be with us. Our house was draughty, not well insulated and had no form of central heating. On one occasion we had a burst pipe in the loft and I remember getting a shock from the water pouring down the light cable. All the lights went out and it was impossible to find the stop-tap outside to cut the water off as this was buried under three feet of drifting snow. Many often sympathise with us about the hot, dusty conditions of the Chaco, but I preferred them to England before the advent of double-glazing and central heating.

Some members of the youth fellowship drew a cartoon with us in the middle of a forest teaching a group of Indians, with the caption, “When I was in England…..” No doubt they were fed up with so many of my stories beginning with, “When I was in Argentina…..”! Maybe another sign that it was time to move on!

As we were travelling by sea, we were encouraged to take everything with us, and we did—including the kitchen fridge! We bought a kerosene Electrolux fridge, an innovation since my boyhood days in the Chaco. We also packed oil paintings of Cromer beach by Rachel's uncle.

We then received a letter from my father, now back in Argentina, which caused us to pause. He questioned the wisdom of my going back to work in the place where I was born and brought up. Had the letter come from anyone else I probably wouldn't have taken too much notice, or else regarded it as the devil's spoke in the wheel to make us doubt our calling. But since it was from my father I felt we ought to take it seriously. I shared it with John Downward, who amongst other good advice, quoted the text, "No man, having put his hand to the plough and looking back, is fit for the Kingdom of God".

Rachel shared the matter with her mother who, without hesitation, quoted the same verse from Scripture. Then we looked at the readings from *Daily Light* for the date we were due to sail, and the same verse appeared again. These three experiences on the same day served to convince us that we should not hesitate, but move forward. Indeed, this text has been a challenge, an incentive and an encouragement to us many times in our life and ministry when faced with change or doubts.

We sailed from Tilbury on 15 September aboard the *RMS Arlanza.* I was appropriately dressed (for those days!) in dark suit and clerical collar. Little Andrew was to celebrate his first birthday on the ship. We were seen off by about 30 well-wishers from Watford, who were allowed on the ship; this was well before the days of screening and sensitive security checks, and the whole ship seemed to be overrun by young people from the church.

We had amongst our travelling companions others going out as Anglican missionaries, notably Revd Patrick Harris who was to become one of our closest friends and with whom we were to share many happy and amusing times as well as live through many difficulties in the development of the work amongst the Indians of Northern Argentina. Also on board were Philip and Jean Craft, a down-to-earth couple whose simplicity radiated a true humility and made them most acceptable to the Indian culture and lifestyle. The late Frances Robathan was another fellow traveller, on her way to Paraguay where she served faithfully as a nurse amongst the Lengua (Enxet) Indians in the Chaco and later undertook administrative responsibilities in Asunción.

With us too was Helen Sohns, returning to Northern Argentina to continue her nursing ministry. Helen had suffered many uncertainties in her young life. Born in Penang of German parents, she spent her early years in Hamburg, from where she was evacuated to a small village away from the bombing. As with all children over the age of ten, she was obliged to join the Hitler Youth. Her mother died during the war and her father soon after. At the age of 17 Helen had to look after her ten-year-old sister. When her godmother took over this care, Helen was able to study nursing in Hamburg and later move to Britain where, after further training, she qualified as a midwife and offered to serve as a nurse in South

America. In the Chaco she became much involved in attending the sick and needy and was fully committed to programmes of preventive medicine. She helped train Wichi and Toba nursing orderlies, whose qualifications gained recognition from the Argentine Ministry of Health. Another of her many achievements was the selection and training of traditional midwives whose presence in the villages enabled expectant mothers to be cared for and give birth in their traditional manner, yet with the addition of improved antiseptic conditions and access to other help if necessary.

The presence on board of colleagues provided opportunity for Christian fellowship and times for Bible reflection, although having a baby to look after meant that Rachel and I were not as regular as we would otherwise have been.

The 21 days of our journey afforded an opportunity for rest and recreation after the rush of packing and emotional goodbyes to family, in Rachel's case her parents, sister and brother, in mine just my sister Cristina since my parents and sister Dorothy were in Argentina. I endeavoured to give my new colleagues some help with basic Spanish, but without immediate success.

Cocoa the Captain

We enjoyed the activities on board and our small group shone in the sports and competitions. Pat Harris as Shakespeare was a highlight in the fancy dress, though the clear winner was Helen Sohns as a *gaucho*, complete with a tanned complexion achieved by smearing her face in cocoa. Unfortunately, when she had the honour of dancing with the captain, the cocoa came off on his pristine white tropical uniform!

Rachel and I represented 'The first day at St Trinian's', myself as mother and Rachel with plaits and school tunic as my young, unwilling daughter. Phil and Jean were postman and parcel!

There was one passenger who prided himself on being on his "fourth missionary journey" *en route* to Vigo in Spain. Each trip had lasted but a few weeks since he declared himself to be a member of the 'Bottle and Polythene Bag Missionary Society'. His method of evangelism was to roll up strips of paper with the text of John 3.16 written in as many languages as possible, place them in a small bottle or polythene bag, and throw them overboard from the ship, trusting they would be washed up on some shore and be picked up by someone ambling along. We called into question the credibility of such a practice and were privately amused at the existence of folk with such eccentricities. Yet, as Bishop Cyril Tucker of Argentina often said when confronted by such a situation, "by all means save some"!

The luggage labels supplied by the Royal Mail Lines afforded me a good sermon illustration. Personal luggage kept in the cabin was marked rather pompously as "STATE ROOM: Luggage accessible on all occasions". The slightly heavier luggage placed in the Baggage Room was labelled "BAGGAGE ROOM: Luggage available on certain occasions". A timetable was announced permitting access to luggage in the Baggage Room so that summer clothes could be got out and winter ones put away, or for belongings to be rearranged. The really heavy luggage was marked "HOLD:

Not wanted on voyage", and was placed in the depths of the ship's hold.

I have likened these labels to people's attitude to God: either He is a reality and accessible on all occasions, or held at arm's length to be resorted to only on special occasions, or else people may blatantly not want Him on the voyage of life, and label Him so…. "Not wanted on voyage."

South America, seen at last

The sighting of the Christ of the Corcovado overlooking Rio de Janeiro signalled we were nearing South America. Our voyage had been full of relaxation and fun, including the 'crossing of the line' and a visit from Father Neptune. Now with just five or six days' sailing to Buenos Aires, we were making preparations to disembark, after shore visits to Rio, Santos and Montevideo, where many years earlier I had seen the top of the mast of the *Graf Spee* before it sank deeper into the mud.

I had been able to renew my Argentine passport, and Rachel had been told initially that as she was married to an Argentine citizen there was no need for a visa. This information was changed just a few days before we sailed from Tilbury, when she was told that she did need a visa. It was by then too late to obtain one, so I asked whether, as the wife of an Argentine, she could be issued with an Argentine passport. The Argentine Consulate accepted the proposal, and a few days before sailing we rushed to London and were issued with the said passport. In the course of the formalities Rachel had to give her fingerprints no less that 80 times!

In Montevideo the Argentine Immigration and Customs authorities boarded and examined all passengers' documentation before the ship docked in Buenos Aires next morning.

The River Plate is the widest river in the world, called by the early colonists the *Mar Dulce* (Sweet Sea). As you approach Buenos Aires, the highest building of that time, the Kavanagh Building, stands out as a clear landmark. In later years I was to pass it daily as I commuted to the Diocesan Office during my 12 years as Bishop of Argentina. Little did I dream of that when we arrived in Buenos Aires in October 1963! The tugboats and other support boats came out to meet the liner and pull and edge her safely to final moorings and journey's end.

It was a great joy to look over the deck rail and see my parents and my sister Dorothy standing on the dock to greet us. This was the first time they had seen their grandson and nephew Andrew. It seemed ages until we were able to disembark, greet my family and face final immigration formalities and customs. This involved examination of all our luggage and household goods. We then had to arrange for these to be transported to the rail terminal for onward journey north.

After negotiating these formalities, Rachel, Andrew and my parents left by taxi for Lomas de Zamora where arrangements had been made for us to stay. This was Rachel's first encounter with Argentina, and when my parents dropped her at the house she suddenly found herself *incommunicado*, unable to understand or make herself understood by the people who received her.

Dorothy and I arrived later by train, a half-hour journey from the centre of Buenos Aires. It was a nostalgic experience, renewing my acquaintance with the smells, cobbled streets and familiar surroundings of Lomas de Zamora where I had spent 10 years at school. So many things had happened in the years I had been away, and many exciting adventures awaited us as Rachel and I began our new life and ministry together in Argentina.

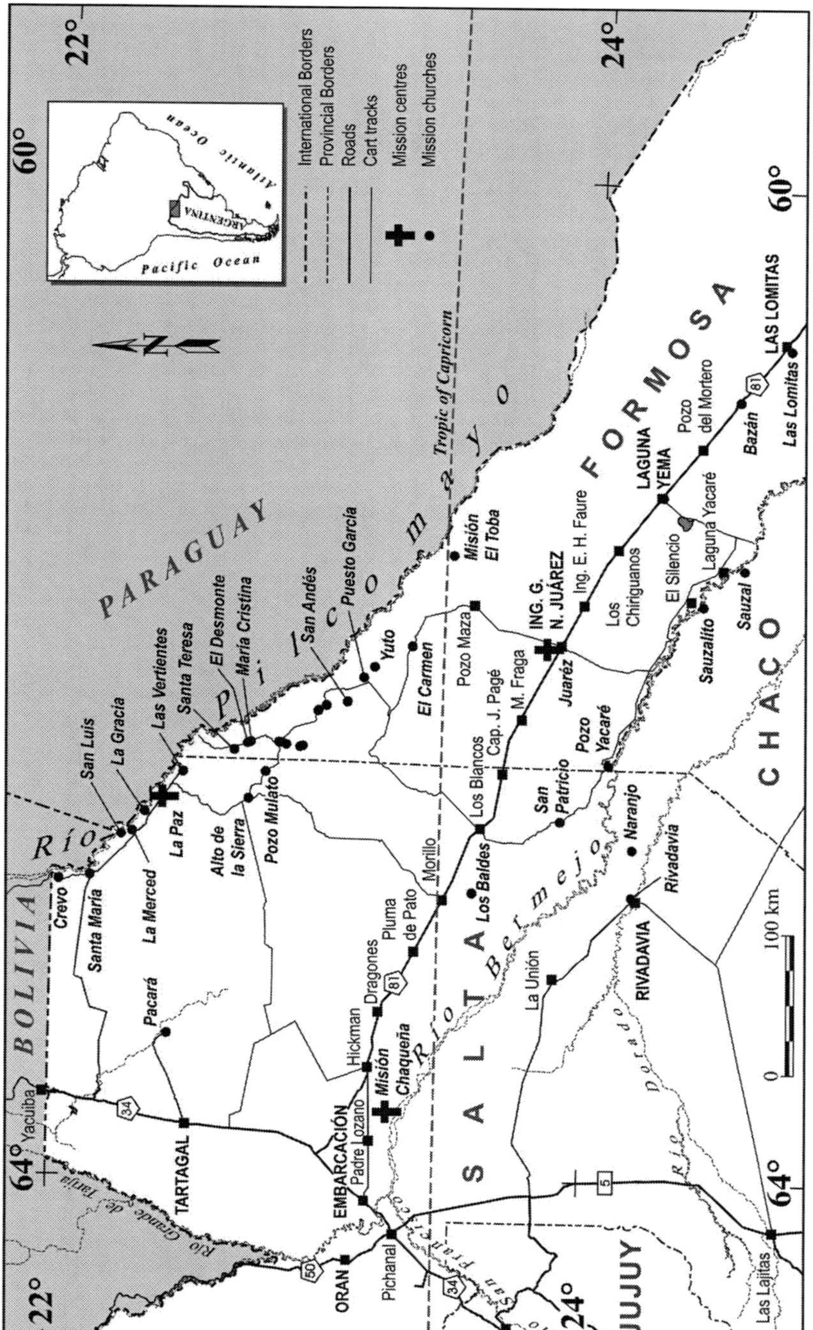

Early Anglican Mission centres and church congregations
Source: Adapted from Grubb, H.C. (1965) *The Land Between the Rivers*, Lutterworth press
Map by Enrique O. López

16

Chaco bound!

AFTER a few days in Buenos Aires, we reserved tickets and sleepers on the train which would take us on the long journey to Salta and Embarcación, where we would change for the last part of the journey to Ingeniero Juárez. For me, it was a kind of *déjà vu* experience, but although I had been this way many times before, I saw it now through different eyes with a wife and child.

There were the same old wooden carriages and sleeping coaches with the *camarero*, steward, responsible for each coach; bunk beds, washbasin, even a potty, a small dresser with mirror and a sluggish fan, glass windows and shutter.

The train, the *Cinta de Plata*, left platform 9 at Retiro Station at 18.30, passing through the northern suburbs of Buenos Aires before branching off towards Rosario and the north. Once out of the urban areas, wide expanses of agricultural countryside took over the view.

The chief waiter from the dining coach would walk the length of the train announcing that dinner would be served and taking table reservations. If there was a great demand, a second sitting was arranged. The journey took me back to the days when I used to travel to and from school. Very little had changed; even the cage where the chickens were kept was still under the dining coach. Only now the train was hauled by two diesel engines instead of steam.

As night fell, the steward would close all the windows and shutters as it was not unknown for stones to be thrown at the train as it passed through the stations. Moving from one coach to the next was quite an adventure. You had to hold firmly to the bars to pass from one carriage's platform to the next. These platforms were reminiscent of those from which American presidential candidates used to greet constituents on their electioneering whistle-stop tours in the far west.

The regular da-da-da-dá of the wheels eventually lulled you to sleep after a last look out of the window to watch the sun sink over the horizon. We travelled through the Province of Córdoba, then across the salty sandy flats of Santiago del Estero, and on to Tucumán, the 'Garden of the Republic', set amidst sugar cane plantations. Further north we had to change trains in Salta, Güemes and Embarcación. Here, on the platform of this one-horse town now referred to as a city, Rachel met her first Mataco Indians and I felt I was coming home. Kevin Bewley, an Australian missionary who was to prove a great friend in the years to come, drove in from Misión Chaqueña, 25 miles away, to greet us and spend some time with us as we waited for the evening train to Ingeniero Juárez, our final destination.

For Rachel this last part of the journey to Juárez felt like penetrating further and further into the forest. The stations are spaced at about 15 miles from each other and all look similar, with bottle trees planted alongside the platform. The train's arrival was a social occasion for the small towns, with everyone turning out to see and be seen, the station staff looking formal in their caps, and town Indians hanging around in the shadows, sadly chewing coca and waiting to pick up any fag end thrown to the ground. The platforms were barely lit with a paraffin pressure lamp shrouded in a cloud of mosquitoes and other insects.

The train usually ran about six hours late; it was scheduled to arrive in Juárez during the night, but we arrived well after daylight. We were met at the station by Walter Robbins with a wheelbarrow. It was raining and it would have been impossible to get to the station with a truck even if he had one!

Walter's responsibility in Juárez was the construction of the houses. Rachel and I with Andrew were allocated to the big house, which we were to share with Barbara Kitchin and Lois Cumming. Barbara was in charge of the educational programme and producing reading primers, whilst Lois was responsible for the medical work. This consisted of hands-on attention for the sick and injured, especially when visiting the Indian villages, but Lois' main thrust was in the area of preventive medicine, the attention and care of TB patients, and continually prodding the government to assume responsibility for medical attention amongst the Indians, who up to that time were given no consideration or care whatsoever.

The three bedrooms of our new home opened to a large room which ran the length of the house. The design was the type seen in the Australian outback. Built of adobes with corrugated sheeting on the roof and no ceiling, it was extremely hot, with little privacy for us as a family or for the other two occupants.

There were no flush lavatories, and a central 'long drop' loo had been built in the middle of the compound equidistant from the three houses. Later, each house had its own 'long drop' similar to those described in *The Specialist*, a book which describes the amenities at the time of the opening up of

Our first home in Juárez

the American west. We had to make use of the loo at a time when there were no Indian visitors waiting to be attended. Otherwise the walk turned into a kind of obstacle race or, at best, was interspersed by a series of chats and conversations because you would be accompanied on the way! Rachel was terrified the children would fall down the 20 metre drop, so they had to be accompanied until they were big enough not to fall through the hole in the seat.

The mission houses were built in a wire-fenced enclosed extent of land on the outskirts of the town, about a kilometre from the station. The land had belonged to a Syrian immigrant called José Jaube who had sought to establish a *palo santo* distilling project. The land had been completely cleared of trees and contained only a well (the attraction for the purchase of the land) and an old steam engine with three distilling tanks.

The project had never been a success. After selling, Jaube chose to live just outside the main gate in a wooden shack. He was one of the local characters: he always wore his trousers rolled up to his knees but seldom wore a shirt, leaving his skin completely tanned. He spoke Spanish with a distinctly Arab accent. Being well versed in basic mechanics, he had often acted as driver to local storekeepers when I was a boy, so I had known him since those days.

Although Jaube had no furniture except for an old bed, table and chair, he did have a kerosene fridge and always kept a row of used peach tins full of water on the shelves. Anyone who visited him or was passing by in the heat of the day was provided with a drink.

He had a number of succinct sayings, including "*El agua ante todo*" (Water before all else) and "*No se puede mezquinar el agua*" (You can't be mean with water).

This was particularly relevant as there were many times in Juárez when our well was the only source of water, and in the hot dry season people would come seeking water at all times of day and night. I was sometimes reluctant to allow them free access to the well as it could leave us without water. We could have resorted to rationing, but undue use of the pump would have damaged it, so I would remember and be mentally reprimanded by Jaube's wise saying!

The pump initially was worked by the steam engine, but this had been replaced by an old diesel engine. Finally, when this no longer functioned, we replaced it with a long extended handle and pumped water by hand.

Juárez, centre of the world

The earlier pioneering work undertaken by Anglican missionaries had established missions amongst the Toba and Mataco Indians along the banks of the Pilcomayo and Bermejo rivers. When we returned to the area, my parents still lived at the Toba Mission, about 55 miles north of Juárez. This was the second location because the first was destroyed by floods. It was situated within easy walking distance of the river and shaded by old algarrobo trees. Though not as extensive as the original mission, its buildings served the community well. The church doubled as a school, there were two buildings set apart as dwellings, a small store, a workshop, and a room constructed on palm tree pylons to be used in the event of any further flooding, which did indeed happen later.

Our being located in Juárez was the implementation of a new mission strategy based around three centres, as described in the next chapter. This strategy was partly to enable the Indian leaders to develop and take initiatives without the presence of the missionary. In the case of Juárez, the personnel at the mission centre were able to give the Indians moving into the small railway town the guidance and 'know how' to take advantage of the albeit small and erratic government services for the sick in the rural hospital and the children in the state school.

Home again!

For me to live again in Juárez was like coming home. One of the features of life there was to act as a sounding board for the Indians who had come to live on the outskirts or made regular visits. Such visits could be for health reasons, or to seek to comply with some legal demand from the government, or to redress a wrong with regard to land rights, or for an unending list of other needs, both material and spiritual. There were few times in the day when there was not someone at the door with some need.

Many arrived by train, which in those days passed through twice a week in each direction. Others just turned up by lorry or tractor and trailer. All was unprogrammed, so it was impossible to set a routine or timetable. This unstructured lifestyle based around the unexpected was to my liking. It was also difficult to plan long-term since the weather was uncertain, especially in the rainy season. The availability of a truck was uncertain too, as was getting the necessary petrol.

When we arrived in 1963 Juárez was a town of about 3,000 with two main stores, one originally owned by the Arab, Jaluf, the other by a Spaniard, Vidal. These had now passed to their sons and family, although Doña Sara, Jaluf's widow, still kept an eagle eye on all the customers from her chair. She was highly skilled in adding up the accounts, and after these had been done on a calculator she would go through them again in her head to make sure no mistake had been made! Prices often depended on the customer, not so much on his economic possibilities, but rather on his ability, awareness of values and courage to question. Often when her son Salomón shouted to her for the price of some article, she would reply, "Who's it for?" Sadly, this meant that the Indians and other humble and innocent folk were often highly overcharged.

As I already spoke Toba, it was felt by those responsible that I ought to make a serious attempt with Rachel to learn the

Mataco language. Rachel has always regretted that she did not also learn Toba, but besides the Mataco language she did pick up Spanish, not the easiest of things to do in Juárez with its northern Formosa accent influenced by the Paraguayan Guaraní language. The general Spanish-speaking population of country peasants were not all that helpful since they could not understand that anyone could speak anything other than Spanish. Though on one occasion one of them obviously did grasp that there were other languages than Spanish, and said to a missionary colleague of mine, "You know, David can speak in Toba, Spanish, English, North American, Australian, and Canadian!" So I came off well!

Barbara Kitchin was delegated to teach us Mataco and found Rachel a model student. My colleagues tell me that I imitated the sounds as I had been familiar with them as a boy, and that I made myself understood by speaking basic Spanish, just placing the Mataco word *häp* between every five words. *Häp* was defined by one Mataco language helper as "a little word that you place in the middle".

17
Despatched to the river

TO DEEPEN our study of Mataco and to understand something of their culture, my father decided we should spend some months on our own by the river at Misión San Andrés. This would place us physically and culturally within the context of a Mataco village and out of reach of any Spanish or English speakers.

San Andrés was the first mission outpost founded by my father and Colin Smith in 1927 when they had been chosen by Richard Hunt to make the exploratory trip to the Pilcomayo river. My uncle Henry Grubb and my Aunt Olive had also lived there. The Indians were used to a missionary presence and had some understanding of the ways of the *wajchäs*, as the white European missionaries were called.

The local church leader was Alberto González, one of the most intelligent and capable Matacos I have ever met. He was Henry Grubb's helper in the first endeavour to translate the New Testament into Mataco (Wichi). He was also one of the first Matacos to own a bicycle. I recall how impressed my father was at the way Alberto mastered the art of centring a wheel, exerting the right pressure on each spoke so there was no wobble as the wheel spun evenly on its axle. One day he carefully set aside valuable ball bearings, only to see the pet roadrunner swiftly pick them up and swallow them. He tied the bird up and patiently waited until they worked through its digestive system, being rewarded with perfectly clean and shiny bearings!

He later directed his attention to car mechanics. On one

With Pastor Alberto González

journey, when miles from assistance, we had trouble with the steering because the ball and socket were badly worn. Alberto suggested we change the position of the socket, move the worn side away from the point of greater pressure, and then wire it all firmly together. By following his advice and proceeding very slowly, changing direction as little as possible, we made it home.

Although he never had the opportunity to drive, he was a brilliant guide and companion on the road, especially in wet weather. Whenever I travelled with him, I abdicated all idea of how to get through the mud and water, implicitly obeying his every word, which always saw us through. He seemed to know exactly what the truck was capable of. When we were stuck, he would give clear commands when to go forward, then back, fill in the track with sticks, logs and weeds, and then guide us forward as far as possible before reversing and repeating the operation. It was often slow progress, but I could not have had better assistance.

Our time in San Andrés preceded the days when motorised transport was available to us. My father took us there in a jeep and when he left us for two months our only means of transport was a *sulky*, a light, large-wheeled mule-drawn vehicle with room comfortably for two.

We made a number of journeys as far as Puesto García and El Yuto, Mataco villages to the east by the river. Rachel adapted marvellously to living with the basics and looking after a one-year-old. In Puesto García, we camped in the small mud and wattle-built church and made our fire on its floor. I slept on one of the pews, while Rachel and Andrew had a camp bed. We had to be up early in the morning as the bell was rung for prayers.

We were the constant object of interest from the Indian children, who hung around all day watching us, as did some adults. They were especially fascinated by Rachel feeding and looking after Andrew and then playing with him.

For me, this lifestyle was reminiscent of my early childhood and very enjoyable, but for Rachel it must have presented many difficulties, with neither toilets nor running water and a fire on the floor. Our menu consisted of fish and goat meat, with pumpkin and sweet potatoes, supplemented by tinned sardines or corned beef with boiled rice.

Famine—then fish aplenty

Our three months in San Andrés coincided with a difficult time for the Indians. There was little food and the fish were slow to appear; there were suspicions that a trap had been built across the river further downstream by the Chunupí tribe, preventing the fish from swimming upstream. Older people would come round after dark to ask for food; dogs were skeletal and weak.

Suddenly, a sound like the low throb of a distant motorboat! The fish were coming at last! At the sound, men and dogs left the village and headed for the river, carrying their nets over their shoulders and extra string and other basic necessities in their *yicas* (string bags). Some then stood shoulder to shoulder in the water, nets held open in scissor fashion with the tips touching the muddy bottom, whilst others from a distance of maybe 100 metres started moving towards them, beating the water with long poles and frightening the fish towards the nets.

A few hours later the men began to return to the village almost overburdened with fish, their *yicas* full, and more fish slung across their shoulders. After months of near famine there was suddenly an over-abundance of food! Dogs that remained in the village too weak to follow their masters to the river greeted them as they returned home. Fires were kindled and soon the smell of roasting fish was omnipresent as smoke wafted across the village. At church next morning there was an unmistakable odour of clothing impregnated with smoke and greasy fish. On arrival at any village you can tell by the smell and the state of the dogs whether fish have arrived or not!

The sharing of the fish showed clearly how far family connections extend. When the men arrive home laden, women from other huts come and sit cross-legged around the perimeter space of their compound. No word is spoken and the women sit patiently until the returned fisherman or a member of his family walks over to one of them and hands her a fish. The recipient expresses no gratitude, nor does the giver expect any; it is a culture with no word for ‘thank you’. The woman receives the fish and walks silently back home.

I noticed that one woman, who had been sitting waiting for quite a long time, was not given a fish and left empty-handed. I later understood that she was considered to be beyond the limits of that particular extended family and therefore not eligible. I also noted that one young boy who had probably returned from his first fishing expedition had so many demands made on his catch by his extended family that by the time his mother returned to the village he had no fish left to show for his first endeavour.

Whilst there may be no word for ‘thank you’ in the ethnic languages of Northern Argentina, this does not imply lack of gratitude. In a sharing culture, these folk have long memories and one good deed is remembered and rewarded in kind at the appropriate time.

Who decides?

We had to learn and grasp the intricacies of the family network, understand who were the decision makers and the folk who had the power to bring about a consensus when difficult decisions had to be taken in the community. We had to be aware of what could and could not be shared: what was personal property and what pertained to the whole community.

These are areas where Christian missionaries need to be particularly sensitive. I have seen entire projects fail because insufficient study was made of the community and family structure before they were introduced. In one instance, three tractor drivers were appointed from the same extended family, thus causing jealousy and eventual failure of the project. In another, four translators were chosen from one community, a decision which could have meant that the Bible texts translated might be rejected by other communities on the grounds of different word usage or pronunciation.

Words and bonds

Our three months in San Andrés were very profitable. We were immersed in the Mataco language and whilst our vocabulary was relatively small, the fact that we were constantly hearing the language, particularly from the children as they played with Andrew, provided us with a good base. We also bonded well with the community, gaining some understanding of their hopes and aspirations. It was probably the last time that the Matacos within the Ingeniero Juárez zone of influence had missionaries resident amongst them.

The work of the Anglican Mission amongst the ethnic groups of Matacos and Tobas was entering a new stage in its development, 40 or so years on since the first missionaries had arrived from Misión Chaqueña.

Such a great salvation

The work initiated in 1911 in San Pedro, moving its centre to

Misión Chaqueña three years later and then reaching out to the Mataco and Toba villages by the rivers Pilcomayo and Bermejo, is one of the outstanding stories in Christian mission. It is no exaggeration to say that it has resulted in the saving and increasing of ethnic groups of Indians who were being decimated by white men's diseases, as well as being chased and persecuted by cattle and land speculators ravaging their traditional homelands and constantly endangering their subsistence lifestyle.

The presence of the missionaries resulted in the valuing of the Indians as people created in the image of God. It has meant provision of medical help for the sick, education of the new generations, advocacy work in helping them recognise and fight for their rights, the valuing of their language and culture, and enabling them to understand the reality of that other culture which surrounded and threatened to envelop them.

Until the early 1960s the pattern of mission activity was based on the traditional style, with missionaries living in the Indian villages and their presence unashamedly paternalistic. It was common to hear them spoken of as "our Indians" and the missionary would spring quickly to their defence if they were seen to be exploited, as well as giving medical attention and visiting when ill or in need. The missionary also exercised a policing role to ensure children were sent to school and the villages were kept clean and tidy; theft was investigated and culprits identified. The life of the community revolved around the missionary-established timetable, punctuated by regular ringing of the bell for prayers, school, opening of the store or dispensary.

It is easy to be critical or regard such activities with superior bemusement. Yet a similar pattern can be seen in the care of parents for their own children: there are times in their development when the parents' role is to be paternalistic; later the children enter other phases, including adolescence, when they become critical of their parents. Further on is the stage of adulthood and maturity when children and parents become friends.

It is important to be aware of these stages in the development of relationships and to respond sensitively to the expectancy of the Indian people. I shall never forget a Mataco, in the course of a conversation, referring to me as "*owuk*", roughly translated "my boss". When I replied, "I am not your boss. I am like you and I am a brother", the look on his face was of pained bewilderment. Until then he had worked and related to me within a social structure he understood and was happy to accept. Now he did not know where he stood. His relational structure had crumbled.

Such changes need to be sensitively dealt with and clearly explained, otherwise people don't know where they stand. Initially one must act and relate to people according to their expectancy, or the community can become dysfunctional.

New missionaries, new ideas

When Rachel and I arrived in Northern Argentina, the Revd Francis Tompkins and his wife Jean headed up the work of the Anglican Mission from the centre in Misión Chaqueña. Francis was the son of my father's colleague, the Revd Alfred Tompkins, and was fluent in Mataco, having been brought up with his brothers Norman and John in Misión Chaqueña amongst the Mataco children, just as I had amongst the Tobas.

Juárez was the second centre, and the third point of the triangle was Misión La Paz by the Pilcomayo river, a centre which served the Mataco, Chorote and Chunupí missions to the north-west. The new strategy responded to the fact that the older missionaries, who had become legendary in the minds of the Indians, were no longer present. My parents, who were bracketed in this category, had returned after a few years in England and provided a kind of on-going succession linking the old days with the new. The arrival of new missionaries with new ideas called for a new way of working, as did the fact that the Indians were now able to read and write, had their own spiritual leaders and teachers, and were more competent in Spanish.

It was decided that each centre should be staffed by missionaries who would focus on areas of particular need in the zone covered. The Indians would have access to help and encouragement through regular missionary visits, including an ordained priest to celebrate the sacraments. This particular issue was to be addressed in the next stage of development of the church. The absence of resident missionaries would place more responsibility on the Indians and allow each church and community, under its own spiritual leader and group of advisors, to decide its own style of development.

18

Advocacy and guidance

THE POLICE station was one of the few buildings of brick and mortar in Juárez and was situated near the main street. A large section of the complex was occupied by the *pajarera*, the birdcage as it was called, where those arrested were initially detained. This large structure was open to the gaze of every passer-by and was where I often visited Indians who were detained. I well remember the irony of a large plaque which hung there bearing the words of the National Anthem, notably the line *"¡Libertad! ¡Libertad! ¡Libertad!"* The irony was not lost on me, but would have been on the mainly illiterate detainees.

When in due course I had the use of a four-wheel-drive jeep, one of the few vehicles in town, I would often be asked by the police to take them to the scene of some incident or to fetch someone who had been wounded or detained. It was good public relations to accede to these requests since it helped place the Indians in a better position, drawing the attention of the police to the fact that there were those who served as their advocates and who would stand up for their cause and rights. Helping the police and maintaining a working relationship with them meant they were less likely to run roughshod over the Indians; and if they did, we had a bargaining chip in our favour in pleading their cause.

Often an arrested Indian with little or no knowledge of Spanish would be at a loss to explain what had happened or to understand what was involved in making a statement or being asked to place his thumbprint at the end of a typewritten document. A detainee could find he'd placed his affirming print to something which could incriminate him without his having understood any of the procedure.

The work of advocacy on behalf of the Indians took up considerable time. It was such matters involving the local and provincial governments, as well as the national government, that made me realise that God had fitted me for this role. My Argentine nationality and my fluency in Spanish, both natural or accidental gifts in human terms, served often to confirm that I was undertaking the work and using the talents that God had given me. I have to admit that I also revelled in the polemics and dialectic involved, as well as walking the corridors of power in government offices advocating Indian rights and challenging the government.

"Show me a man ..."

Missionary activity amongst the Indians had its beginnings in the Chaco in 1914, and led to the proclamation of the Gospel and the founding of a Church with its own baptised and confirmed members and local leaders. These leaders were known as evangelists, and in the main were men of deep spirituality and moral ascendancy in their communities; most of them, however, were illiterate since they were usually the older men.

Bishop Daniel Ivor Evans would travel to the missions from Buenos Aires as and when possible, and was very sympathetic to the work, enjoying his visits. But he was quite clear that the Indians should not be ordained. His concept of Church and its leadership was that an ordained priest should be able to serve anywhere within the wider Anglican Commu-

On the Provincial Salta-Formosa border

nion, something the Wichi and Tobas would certainly not be able to do. It did not seem to occur to him that conversely anyone ordained in Ely or Canterbury would not automatically be fitted or qualified to minister in the Chaco!

It was not until his successor, Bishop Cyril Tucker, came on the scene that momentous changes took place. He had strong links with the British and Foreign Bible Society and the Church Missionary Society, and prior to his consecration had been Vicar of Holy Trinity, Cambridge. He came with a completely different approach to the mission of the Church and its leadership. His simple phrase, "Show me a man who can spiritually raise his fellows and I will lay my hands on him" opened a new phase in the development of the Indian Church. The faithful leaders would soon be fully recognised in their ministry; I think Bishop Tucker thought it unlikely they would have to minister in Ely or Canterbury, and was not concerned anyway!

The first to be ordained were the elders of the Church, those faithful evangelists. As to faith and commitment, there was little more one could demand of them: they had already for many years been true pastors in their communities. Brief courses were held for them, together with instruction in how to administer the sacraments. These courses and much of the future preparation of new leaders from a younger generation were undertaken by my father. This was ideal since it could have been interpreted that ordination was the idea of a new bishop or a new generation of missionaries. My father became the link between the early pioneering days of the Church and its growth to maturity with its own ordained leadership. He was present at all the early ordination services and thus had the joy of witnessing the clear fruits of his own ministry and that of his contemporaries. The Indian Church had come of age!

Schools and the wider world

The work of literacy undertaken by Barbara Kitchin, plus the ongoing pressure placed on the government to accept Indians into the state schools and to open schools in the villages, were bearing fruit. Teaching courses were held, as well as courses for the preparation of radio programmes. Barbara prepared much basic literacy material, the best known being *Pepe thaye Ema*. The Chaco was a far cry from her home in Kendal and

Bishop Mario and Rosa, Rachel and I with Indian clergy

schooling and teaching experience in Watford, and her strong wrists enabled her to manoeuvre her vehicle on muddy roads in the wet season. She covered thousands of miles visiting Indian villages and made a huge impact on the work of empowering the poor and providing them with new opportunities and new horizons.

She also opened up opportunities for the Indians to take advantage of courses in the cities of Salta and Buenos Aires. Such opportunities not only served to train new Indian leaders, but also introduced them to the wider Church and to the world of secular government, thus making their needs and the work of the Church better known.

Further excellent work in the education field was achieved by Argentine missionaries Silvia Roitberg and Betty Somoza (now Betty Plumb). Silvia founded a school in Juárez which developed into a large secondary establishment, and Margaret Bates (now Margaret Archer) supervised the creation of a community centre there.

A medical Godsend

Parallel to the work in education was that undertaken in the medical field. The contribution of the first missionaries had been a 'hands-on' ministry to the acutely and chronically ill, often done by people with only basic first aid experience—with the exception of Edward Bernau in Misión Chaqueña and Colin Smith in the Pilcomayo area.

But then Dr Michael Patterson, with his wife Virginia, undertook an exceptional ministry, not only with 'hands-on' medical attention but also constantly badgering the government authorities to assume responsibility for preventive medical attention and overall health care for the Indians. The presence of such a highly qualified medical practitioner was in every sense a Godsend.

Michael is a quiet, conscientious and sensitive person, convinced of his vocation to give his all for the Indians. With an added streak of British eccentricity, he became a well known character, and not only amongst the Indians. He was a person to be contended with when he presented cases to government officials and brought pressure to bear on them. He cut a formidable figure, over six feet tall, with baseball cap and jeans tucked into leather boots and carrying a huge Wichi *yica* overflowing with medical reports and health projects.

In his softly spoken Spanish and Wichi, he would reveal some embarrassing government failure to dark-suited ministers in Government House, or equally comfort a dying Indian in hospital.

At one stage, to make a point and establish a precedent, Michael founded a small clinic in Misión La Paz and the Ministry of Health appointed him as Director. The work there and along the River Pilcomayo came under the immediate oversight of Dr Margaret Scott (later Dr Margaret Lunt), supported by a team of missionary and indigenous nurses. Michael's ultimate objective was to create a post and then vacate it, thus ensuring the government had to make the next appointment.

Michael's period of work as a doctor amongst the Indians is a watershed in medical care for the Indians. The emphasis on preventive medicine has meant an upsurge in the Indian population, a noticeable reduction in cases of TB, and a serious ongoing spraying project to eliminate the *Chagas-Maza* disease (American Trypanosomiasis). This is a parasitic infection endemic in rural areas of Latin America, transmitted by contact with the faeces of the *vinchuca*, also known as the kissing bug. There is a swelling of the eyelid and over the long term the parasites reach and affect the heart and other organs.

Many cases remain undetected until a blood test is done. It was a surprise when such a test was done on me in Misión Chaqueña and proved positive. I must have contracted it when I was a child since the rest of the family proved negative. As a boy I remember Dr Maza's visits to us looking for *vinchucas*;

we used to collect them in little boxes, unaware of the possible repercussions from the bites. I am assured by specialists that no lasting damage has been done to my heart, and as Michael Patterson reassuringly said, "You'll always prove positive to *Chagas* but in all likelihood will live to well over 90 and die of the flu." So I've not worried about it since, though I did submit to a test at the Malbran Institute in Buenos Aires in 1982, during which I was tested by bites from sterile *vinchucas*; if they contracted *Chagas* from me, then I was definitely infected! Unfortunately, the experiment was interrupted by the South Atlantic War and I had to get back to my family in Salta.

Virginia Patterson was a true helpmate to her husband Michael. Her jovial personality, ready laugh and loving concern for all, whatever time of day or night she was called upon, was proverbial. A good speaker of Spanish and Mataco, she was able to help in the education programmes as well as taking a deep concern in areas of social and economic aid, giving much time to the buying and selling of Indian crafts. She suffered from the heat and dust of La Paz, yet soldiered on, no doubt often wondering how such a wilderness had replaced for her the lovely homes in Iver, Buckinghamshire, where the Duke of Kent's family grew up and Cheltenham Ladies College where she taught. The development of the Church and its outgoing concern in the educational and medical fields owe much to women who sacrificially gave their lives to work among the Indians. Those who were married had particular problems in bringing up their children in a hostile and difficult environment and an alien culture and language, as well as coping with the excessive heat and mosquitoes, whilst attending to the many needs of the Indians who came to the door, totally oblivious to the stress and strains that these mothers were facing.

The single women had added frustrations, often having to share a house with colleagues with whom they were not compatible, separated from their families and often forfeiting the possibility of finding a partner. They were completely dedicated to their calling, and the particular group with whom our period of work coincided were magnificent, highly qualified professionals who could well have made their mark in responsible posts in their own countries.

In nursing, Lois Cumming, who sadly has since died, made a particular contribution in the Province of Formosa. A highly qualified British nurse, she yet had to revalidate her qualifications to make a true and academically recognised contribution in Argentina. She faced this challenge resolutely, having initially to complete the Argentine Secondary and then the University Nursing Course qualifications. This all gave her added status when she challenged the Provincial Ministry of Health to assume responsibilities for the medically marginalised Indians.

One of the first tasks that Lois undertook was to evaluate the true situation with regard to the many who suffered from TB. She visited each village, carried out a census of the population, and took sputum tests. Equipped with this information, she faced the Minister of Health. When impediments and queries were placed in her way, she responded with the survey she had made.

"We do not know how many Indians there are."

"I do," said Lois.

"We do not know how many cases of TB there are."

"I do," she would reply, producing her statistics. Lois was not someone who would take "No" for an answer.

Soon drugs and milk were included in the government budget and distributed to the Indians, as well as added food rations. I once met an Indian who was disappointed that he had not been diagnosed with TB as he wanted a food ration!

Lois fought hard for the Indians to be accepted and treated in the local hospital in Ingeniero Juárez. Few appointments were allocated to them each day, and they were fearful of going to the hospital. They trusted the British nurses, but feared the hospital staff, who in general were antagonistic to them.

Lois and her colleagues saw the need to put pressure on the local hospital to accept Indian patients, and encouraged the Indians to be less fearful and accept treatment there. This meant discouraging what she called "having medical consultations and dispensing at the kitchen door". Unfortunately, for some of the Indians this necessarily strict line was misinterpreted as a lack of love and sympathy. I remember the case of a small child with very bad eyes. I convinced Lois, against her better judgment and policy, to attend to the child outside our house. She placed drops speedily into one eye and before I could tell her they were also required in the other eye she was ten yards away speeding back home! She did return and attended the other eye; overall, though, her strict line had positive results.

The hospital in Juárez is today attended mainly by Indians, a priority reflected in the bilingual notices all around. Many of the nursing staff are Indians too. The determined work of missionaries in areas of literacy and nursing have borne fruit, enabling the Indians to become responsible for their own needs and problems and to become part of the solution.

Third World Roman Catholics

In the early 1970s, a wave of socially conscious left-wingers began to infiltrate the established structures of the government and NGOs. The first of these to arrive in Juárez, together with some 'Third World Priests', were initially aggressive and critical of the Anglican work. In fact, they commandeered the San Andrés mission which at the time had no resident missionary.

With the passing of the years, this new group moderated and, having had close contact with the Indians and their culture, began to view the decades of Anglican presence with different eyes. I recently met one of the priests who candidly told me that had he contacted the Anglican Church first he would have become an Anglican!

In fact, there was little proselytising and priests and nuns accepted the established Anglican Church as the Church of the Indians, even attending Holy Communion services, whilst they threw their efforts into social action and became a thorn in the side of the government as they questioned its failure to attend to the Indians as they should. Maybe their presentations and political pressures were weightier than ours as coming from the majority Church in Argentina. Over the years, a greater friendship and confidence has been established and recently much work concerning the Indians has been undertaken together.

The happy and positive relationship between the Director of the Juárez Hospital and the missionary nursing staff is clearly seen in the incorporation of nurses Helen Sohns, Kirsten Walker, Beryl Gilbert and Fiona Ross (who sadly died in a traffic accident) on to the medical staff.

Helen's main responsibility was the training of what came to be known as Traditional Midwives, with a local woman trained to be the midwife in her community. Birth would take place in the hut following the traditional ways of childbirth, in a sitting position rather than lying; only where there was uncertainty would the mother-to-be be transferred to the hospital. Traditional methods were followed, but incorporated antiseptic conditions where necessary and appropriate.

Kirsten, who came to Argentina with much enthusiasm and youthfulness, was from a medical missionary family, her father being a doctor who had worked in the Middle East. Her responsibilities were for babies and children, and she undertook an intensive programme of child care which involved visiting the villages, examining the babies, keeping a record of their development and providing extra milk where necessary. It was always a community event when the babies came together and were each placed in a weighing machine hung from a branch. They then had the circumference of their upper arms measured, which gave some indication as to nutrition needs.

Beryl, who hailed from Yorkshire and spoke Wichi with a distinct Yorkshire accent, threw all her endeavours into the TB programme, training nurses to take sputum tests and be responsible for the ongoing control and treatment of patients. To have more convenient access to the little consulting room, she arranged for a house to be built as her home in the Wichi village on the outskirts of Juárez.

Many nursing orderlies were trained in the Juárez zone. Susana Somoza, a qualified biochemist who had joined the missionary team from Buenos Aires, transferred to the provincial government payroll and became a full-time member of the hospital staff.

Under the direction of Dr Hilario Ferrero, the government medical team in Juárez set up an extensive and effective programme. It would be true to say—and the Director would be the first to acknowledge it—that such a programme would never have been possible without the early basic attention and training provided by the missionaries. The years prior to the government medical presence were crucial in laying a strong foundation: the pressure exerted on the government to assume responsibility for the Indians' medical care, and the instilling of confidence and dispelling of fears amongst the Indians to break down prejudice and accept this service, had been very effective.

Relief and development

Besides opening the door to the ordination of Indians, Bishop Tucker faced the problem of their social needs. This, added to concern in the 1970s for development and the accessibility to funding for NGOs, resulted in the arrival of new missionaries whose calling was to express the love of Christ in practical ways, develop the making and sale of native crafts, and initiate projects in agricultural development. The next chapter details the optimistic ten-year plan to try to resolve and supplement the increasingly obsolescent style of subsistence living.

With Tobas of the older generation

19

Two firsts

AS I LOOK back over the years, I see two major events in the development of the Indian Church. One already referred to is the ordination of the first Indians as deacons and priests, which culminated in the consecration in 1975 of Mario Mariño as bishop. In fact, this deeply gifted, spiritual man, a natural pastor and servant, was the first Amerindian bishop of the Anglican Communion. The other major event was the translation of the complete Bible into Wichi (*Mataco*)[1], a mammoth task that not only bears witness to God's message and action of salvation for the Wichi in their own language, but also serves to maintain and safeguard the culture of a people and establish the reality and validity of their language. The Christian missionaries, far from destroying a culture, have nurtured and preserved it.

The first work of translation was undertaken by Richard Hunt, followed later by Alfred Tompkins. Not only did they translate selections of the Holy Scriptures, but also produced the first Mataco Prayer Book (1928), an English-Mataco Dictionary and an accompanying Grammar. These first missionaries were not trained linguists, but were endued with much sanctified common sense and sensitivity to the culture and customs of the people, as well as a complete devotion to the task in hand and a clear objective. These early endeavours were followed up by Henry Grubb who, in the midst of many

[1] Over the years *Mataco* has taken on a pejorative sense and has been universally replaced by *Wichi*, the people's own name for themselves and their language.

other responsibilities, worked alongside his Mataco assistant Alberto González to produce the New Testament.

The new generation of missionaries worked on further revisions and complete new translations. Maurice Jones added to his teaching responsibilities and family commitments the translation of selections from the Old Testament. Working in his small home against the background of his children making their demands and with people continually at the door, he seemed to have the concentration and ability to close his mind to everything else and produce his translation. It was very much a personal and individual effort.

The work on the eventual complete Bible in Wichi was taken up by Bob Lunt. Bob is a person endued with deep sensitivity and able to identify completely with the Indian way of seeing things. His silent, non-pushy demeanour and humility enabled him to fit into the reality of Wichi community life, and his understanding of the language made him a Godsend at this moment in the history of the church. His body language and ability to converse fluently in Wichi would make him pass without being noticed, if he were not white with a shock of auburn hair and more often than not wearing a red pullover! He was quickly named *Fwalalä*, the little vermilion flycatcher bird familiar in the Chaco. Bob is also known in the community as 'Don Roberto' and is highly respected because of his linguistic abilities. Since completing the Bible, he has also produced a new Wichi Grammar which has been acclaimed by the University of Salta and is used by students who today are taking a renewed interest in Indian ethnic matters.

Bob worked closely with Wichi helpers, the best known being Isidro Vilte, who knows sufficient Spanish to understand the Spanish Bible and has a thorough understanding of the language and its dialects. His political ambitions and rather mercenary attitude to the work often made life difficult for Bob, but Isidro has a penetrating understanding of translation work, a long historical link with and knowledge of the first missionary endeavours and the objectives of the work.

Isidro comes from a particularly gifted family who have always aspired to and exercised a leadership role in the river Pilcomayo community. This has, however, not always proved positive, since there are critics who regard parts of the translation with some disdain and say, "Oh, those are just Isidro's words!" Bob tried to gain some form of unified consensus with regard to the final translation since the Bible was to cover a wide area in which scattered communities had different dialects and regional variations of vocabulary and pronunciation.

The United Bible Societies' translations consultants work closely with translators in the field, and Dr Bill Mitchell and latterly the Revd Tito Lahaye made regular visits to help ensure accuracy and steady progress. The aim was to produce a version that did not literally translate each word, but captured the sense, adapting to the culture and local circumstances. Translating 'white as snow' when you live in the tropics needs some thinking through, as does 'greet one another with a holy kiss' in a community that is not publicly tactile or given to refined salutations.

After seeing and handling typewritten, dog-eared translations with corrections, and latterly pages and pages of computer-produced work, I found it a moving experience to hold a complete copy of *Dios Lhämtes tä Matchehen* (God's True Words) clearly printed on paper and bound in an impressive black cover. The printers unfortunately printed the illustration of the writing on the wall referred to in Daniel 5.5 the wrong way round, but in the text the words, '*Mene Mene Tekel….*' are correctly translated.

The presentation of the new Bible was a moving occasion. Services were held in Juárez and Santa María, as well as at Misión Chaqueña where the first translation endeavours took place nearly a century before. There was also a momentous event in the Avenida Theatre in Buenos Aires, to which government and civic authorities were invited, for the dedication of "this first complete Bible in a national language of Argentina." Dr Salvador Dellutri, President of the Argentine Bible Society, gave a magisterial address and Isidro Vilte and other members of the team of translators shared in the presentation. It was a moving occasion for Bob Lunt as he held the large presentation copy of the Bible, the fruit of many years' faithful endeavour. What more wonderful legacy could one leave to the Wichi and the Church?

Higher theological orientation

Years before, Maurice Jones had been designated to head up the preparation and training of men for ordination. The 'elder statesmen' and Christian leaders had already been ordained as the first ministers of the Church, but it was now time to look to younger men and their training. Communities where the younger generations were now going to primary school, becoming conversant with Spanish and aware of the wider world, would need clergy who were also alert to these developments and able to minister in an ever changing cultural situation.

Candidates were chosen by their community leaders with a suggested criterion as to the gifts and abilities required. It was made clear that ordination would be considered at the end of the course and that being a pastor in the community would not command a salary. The plan was that each village should have its own pastor who would continue to live there and gain his livelihood in the same manner as his peers, but be the authorised spiritual leader of his people in worship, administering the sacraments, and serving as their teacher and guide.

The course was initially three years. Misión Chaqueña, the established headquarters of the Anglican work, was the place chosen and small one-roomed houses were built to accommodate the students. The family accompanied the candidates, including children up to the age of 18. The year was to be divided into academic terms, giving the families the opportunity of returning home to their villages for vacations.

Maurice Jones was a keen, disciplined Bible student himself and a strict disciplinarian, and he would make it clear if he were not in agreement with something, as those who have been the recipients of his long, spidery written letters will witness.

Although Maurice was not always patient with misdemea-ours, nor with certain elements of the Indian culture, his fair and strict methods of discipline were accepted, understood and respected. His students clearly received a good training and look back to those years with a positive attitude. The Church certainly has much for which to thank Maurice.

Another who made a valuable contribution to the training was Kevin Bewley, a likeable Australian. Stephen Barrett, a fellow-countryman who later made a significant contribution in the area of training, jokingly said to me, "There are two types of Australians: nice ones and nasty ones. I'm one of the nasty ones!"

Kevin was certainly one of the very nice ones and a link with the previous generation of missionaries, having worked with Henry Grubb and Harry Dickson. He was well attuned to the Indian culture and, as a bachelor, could spend many hours with the Indians, sometimes chatting and yarning late into the night around the fire, a time when many of their truths and secrets are revealed.

Kevin came from a practical country background, his father owning a nursery business just outside Sydney. He was the only son among eight children, and this contributed no doubt to his gentlemanly kindness to the many single lady missionaries, although he could be strict when necessary. A demanding Canadian girl hitch-hiker arrived in Juárez, expecting to be cared for and taken around. Kevin contacted one of the oil transporters with whom he arranged for her to continue her journey. His comment afterwards was, "I didn't treat her in any way that I wouldn't have treated my sister."

The Indians loved Kevin, but the need to care for and help

his father made it necessary for him to return to Sydney. Frequent return visits, nonetheless, were much appreciated.

Jeanne Carter was another great asset in the formal training of the Indians at the Bible Institute. She was a qualified teacher and so was able to bring her gifts to bear in providing ideas and courses to help with the teaching of children, and she also gave literacy instruction to the students. Although of a quiet disposition, she would courageously undertake visits to isolated villages, remaining there on her own whilst she carried out her training and teaching ministry.

The Church and work of mission were greatly blessed at this period with well qualified and above all enthusiastic missionaries, many of whom took their share in teaching in the Bible Institute where, besides theological teaching, instruction was given in other areas. I was allocated to help improve Spanish and to give lessons on adaptation, change and understanding the newly enveloping Argentine culture.

Whilst the specific objectives were Christian teaching, translating the Scriptures and training new leaders, emphasis was also placed on seeking ways to complement and improve the poor and precarious lifestyle of the Indians, together with advocacy on their behalf concerning the rights to their traditional lands. The Christian message of a "life more abundant" needs to be reflected in the here and now. Someone once said that it's all very well to promise cake in heaven, but it's important to provide at least a crust on earth!

Maurice Sinclair (later Bishop Maurice) clearly saw the need to implement a complementary practical ministry in seeking to meet the Indians' physical needs and political aspirations. For him this was an intrinsic part of the full expression of the Good News of Jesus Christ. He has outlined his thinking in his book *The Green Finger of God.* Unfortunately it was published on the eve of the unexpected South Atlantic war with the break-up of the largely British missionary team working in the development projects, so that it probably did not receive the reflection it merited.

Latin American theologian Samuel Escobar in his Foreword says about the need for development and relief aid to accompany the work of evangelism and mission: "This is the kind of evangelism that the Bible describes, in contrast to those dualistic spiritualising models that so many evangelistic handbooks have perpetuated in recent decades, and in contrast too to the theological liberationists ..... whose starting point is a jump into Marxist praxis that goes afterwards to the Bible in order to find justification for itself."

The practical outworking of Maurice Sinclair's careful reflection was seen in the newly created arm of the Church, *Iniciativa Cristiana*, which was the Church's expression and response to social concern for the Indians. An integrated programme was outlined for a 10-year period.

This was the missionaries' first coordinated endeavour to help socially. A lot had been done in finding an outlet for native weaving among the Tobas and one of my responsibilities in the mission store during my first job had been the buying and packing of the weaving. The carpentry endeavours initiated by Mr Cecil Everitt became famous throughout Argentina for what was known as the 'Anglican

Chair'. These basic chairs of cedar or algarrobo with rawhide seats were to be seen beside the bed of every boarder at St George's College, as well as in the most outlandish lorry drivers' cafés on the main highways. Medical work, too, had from the earliest days been an integral part of the missionary presence.

The ambitious 10-Year Plan hopefully covered every area of social need, a truly holistic endeavour at resolving the Indians' poverty. On the Argentine media the word *indígena* was usually preceded by *problema*, so in the belief that every problem posed is an opportunity to find a solution, it was a worthy plan.

Maurice Sinclair was accompanied by a highly qualified and gifted team. The development of the project in the early 70s coincided with European governments and ecumenical church organisations having funds to dispense, and if a viable and credible project were presented it was likely to receive funding. *Iniciativa Cristiana* had people able not only to work in the field but also gifted in expressing project needs in writing; they were conscious, too, of the political and Christian leanings of the donor agencies and able to forward appropriate projects to the agency most likely to help.

Efforts were not always crowned with success. Maurice once asked me to accompany him on a tour of commercial companies in Argentina who might be willing to help. After an extensive journey to Mendoza and Buenos Aires, punctuated by several interviews, all we got was a record and some ant powder! Almost 100 per cent of funding came from outside the country.

One of the high profile personalities in the project was Kevin McKemey. Of Irish descent, born to missionary parents who worked in Africa where his first schooling took place, his forefathers founded the Presbyterian Church in the United States and were referred to by a historian as "Reckless but Godly men", qualities that Kevin inherited. Though he had lost some sight in one eye, he was a good, fast driver whose journeys from Misión Chaqueña to Salta and back became proverbial for speed. His wife Denise was endued with extraordinary patience, rarely knowing where he was; at the drop of a hat he would fly down to Buenos Aires or drive to Formosa. On one occasion I had taken my car to Orán to be repaired and was waiting at a crossroads hoping to get a lift home to Juárez about 500km to the east, when Kevin suddenly appeared from the opposite direction on his way to Salta. Without hesitation, he made a u-turn and drove me all the way home!

20

Worlds apart

WHILST the work moved forward in both training of church leaders and relief and development, Rachel and I were in Juárez. Andrew was growing up and enjoyed playing with his friend Stephen Robbins, especially after a welcome rainstorm when they would play in the water and come home covered in mud. Of constant concern to us were the cactus plants that formed a hedge around the house with their long sharp thorns and the badly covered 20 metre deep well. Rachel was expecting our second child and Michael Patterson suggested that because of lack of facilities in Juárez, in the event of any unexpected problems we should travel to Buenos Aires. I felt a bit guilty about this since back in 1935 my mother had faced my birth in a much more remote area without any possibility of pre- or post-natal care.

Arrangements were kindly made by Bishop Cyril and Kathleen Tucker for us to stay with them for the period before and after the baby's birth, which meant about three months away. As well as the great distance between Juárez and Hurlingham, they were poles apart in culture, economics and landscape.

Bishop Tucker looked to me as a kind of valet, chaplain and translator. It was still early days for him and his wife in Argentina and there were details that a lack of Spanish made complicated.

Those were the days when a telephone was obtained at a high premium. In fact, people would actually buy a property if it meant getting a phone line, as this certainly added value.

Rachel with Philip and Andrew by a large cactus

One of the early complications was to get a telephone transferred from one point to another in the house. Bishop Cyril arranged for the Revd Ariel Cristóbal, the first Latin Argentine to be ordained, to sort the matter out. Ariel dutifully went to the telephone exchange, but was unsuccessful since there were problems with the bill, which needed first to be cancelled by the previous owner of the house.

Bishop Cyril thought I might be more successful, so I went and tried diplomatically to resolve the problem of the *Teléfono del Obispado.* In Argentina the Church (albeit confused with the Roman Catholic Church) still carried weight, but even this tack was unsuccessful.

Bishop Cyril, by now experiencing a certain frustration at a problem quite unlike the ones faced at Holy Trinity Vicarage in Cambridge, decided that maybe his own inability to explain his predicament in Spanish might in fact get things moving. So he went himself, but was back in record time, having found the office shut as it was a holiday. It was *el Día del Telefonista*, the Day of the Telephone Operator! This was the first of many frustrations with Argentine bureaucracy.

Other matters also had to be sorted out. The dog became ill, so I accompanied Bishop Cyril to the vet, thinking all the while of the skeletal Indian dogs in the Chaco whose owners could not even see a doctor, let alone a vet for their dog.

Bishop Cyril introduced the matter in his limited Spanish: "*Yo no hablo castellano, mi hamigo habla mucho……*" His pronunciation of '*Yo*' was like 'Joe', so rather naughtily I nicknamed him Joe! The translation of the phrase was, "I do not speak Spanish, but my friend speaks a lot….." He would then elucidate in English: "Please tell him the dog has been sick and quite likely has problems with his kidneys caused by drinking chemically treated water from the swimming pool". I did the translation, the dog was treated and recovered. We had had rather more success than with the telephone!

At a visit to the ironmonger's with the lawnmower, a similar introduction was made: "*Yo no hablo castellano….*", with an explanation of what had happened to the lawnmower. This, too, was repaired.

Cyril had an ongoing tussle with Argentine bureaucracy. Fortunately his sense of humour and great patience, probably learned during his Japanese prisoner of war days, enabled him to live with it and see it in an amusing, objective manner. He told me that if he ever wrote a book about his experiences in Argentina, he already had the title. He said that if a fully laden bus went over a precipice on a winding mountain road, the police would arrive, take a look at the upturned vehicle and the dead and injured around it, and comment, "*No hay problema…*" In Argentina there always seems to be some way round a problem.

Nappies in a Hurlingham bucket

Our son Philip was born at the British Hospital. Rachel was rushed there by Michael Vernon, the Rector of Hurlingham, who for a short time had worked with us in the north. Her blood pressure was extremely high, but the doctor assured her there was nothing to worry about. Rachel told him it was not the birth she was anxious about, rather the terrifying speed she had been driven across Buenos Aires!

When she returned to Hurlingham, Rachel was wondering how to wash and sterilise the nappies. The maid Mariquita was shocked to be asked for a metal bucket and to light a fire on the edge of the lawn to boil them as Rachel did in Juárez. One didn't do that in Hurlingham, so alternative means were found.

Hurlingham is the home of Argentine polo and of the Hurlingham Club, where the expatriate social elite of the British community would relax and farmers coming in from the 'camp' would lodge. There are still many English-speaking residents there with their manicured lawns and uniformed maids. Some ladies came round to the Tuckers' and drinks were served. Rachel was desperately thirsty and accepted a large glass of something still and crystalline believing it to be a soft drink. When her head began to reel, she realised she had inadvertently downed a powerful gin and tonic. She asked to be excused on the pretence that she needed to change Philip's nappy.

Philip gained weight and there were no complications, so we prepared to return to Juárez. Rachel often commented as we visited or flew over Buenos Aires, "Thank God we do not have to live here", although our time with Cyril, Kathleen and their children Rosemary, John and Susan, had been happy. It was also a time which afforded us an opportunity to see, and briefly live, the lifestyle that unbelievably was to be ours in later years.

The Tuckers' lovely home, set in its own large garden with swimming pool, was subsequently sold and they moved to a flat within the city of Buenos Aires. A few years later, this was also sold and a large house bought in Olivos as the bishop's residence. Little did we dream at the time that one day we would be living there and that Hurlingham and its beautiful church would be under my care as bishop.

But back to reality

The time came to take the train from Retiro station and make the return journey to Embarcación, via Tucumán and Salta. It was an exciting moment as we returned with a new baby and we looked forward again to seeing Andrew, who was staying with his grandparents and Auntie Dorothy in Misión Chaqueña. Unwisely, perhaps, we had left Andrew with them without mentioning we were going to Buenos Aires. We had left late one evening when he was asleep and now appeared three months later with Philip. As a kind of compensation prize, we brought him a second-hand red tricycle. It's not surprising that at first he wanted little to do with us, preferring to remain with his grandparents. He soon came round, though, speeding on his tricycle and fascinated by his new little brother. After a while we continued our journey by train home to Juárez.

We soon settled back into the old routine. As Bishop Tucker once commented, living in the Chaco requires you to spend 80 per cent of your time maintaining the fabric of family life, with even basic things like a fire, light and water requiring considerable work and forethought.

Wood had to be bought, usually from the Indian women who would themselves go and chop it, and bring it in on their backs held by a strap or string from their foreheads. Wood was calculated by the piled-up square metre. Like most work undertaken by Indians, the wooding experience was a group affair, spiced by stories, comments and laughter. Once they had unloaded the wood at our house, they would sit around and Rachel would provide *mate* and bread, together with buckets of water to wash their faces and soak their hair. After payment, they would return happily to their village on the outskirts of town.

Water was always an uncertainty. We had our own well but the diesel engine was difficult to start and constantly broke down, so we fitted an extended handle to the pump. This made pumping relatively light and we had men who were pleased for a few pesos to come and pump water regularly for us. It was pumped into a raised tank and underground piping took it to the three houses.

This system was fairly successful and covered basic needs. There were times, however, when I would hear a desperate cry from Lois Cumming or Fiona Ross to say that the water had run out, and more often than not Walter Robbins and I would have to go and pump. This always seemed to occur after dark!

Another problem with the water was that the leather washers in the pump 20 metres down would frequently wear out. This involved calling in Orquera, the well man, who would climb down the well to unscrew the three bolts that held the pump. The main weight of the pipes above it had to be secured first. This was a dangerous and unpleasant job: the deep well had its resident frogs and snakes and was dark and wet. Orquera was adept at the job, when not drunk. The pump had two leather washers; sometimes the right size was available and sometimes not. As one who often had to pump the water and undertake the tasks of maintenance, I realise how precious water is.

Initially, our lighting was with Tilley-type pressure lamps, effective, but hot, noisy, and often difficult and dangerous to light with alcohol and paraffin, especially for Rachel when I was away. Our fridge was also dependent on paraffin; I have yet to understand how a wick and flame can produce ice in a freezer!

Bottled gas arrived in Juárez in due course, making a big difference. The gas lamps gave good light, but also produced a lot of heat and could be noisy, though they were easier for Rachel to manage. The gas also supplemented our wood supply when we were able to acquire a gas stove.

Later, the municipality set in motion the installation of electric generators. These were sited close to the centre of town, the noise a small price to pay for what initially were just a few hours of electricity. This brought change, although the hurried installation of power cables by people with little experience and unaware of the invisible power and danger of electricity brought in its wake some tragedies. An employee was working on the main installation of power cables, when someone turned on the current. The man was hurled three metres to the ground, but survived with a few broken bones and bruises. Others were not so fortunate. One young man died instantly when he leaned against his chicken wire fence. One of the supporting posts housed the electric meter and the constant rubbing of the cables against the fence had worn the insulation causing the entire fence to become live.

The local stores were quick to stock fridges, fans and air

conditioners, although initially current was generated for a few hours only. There were many problems—no regular supply of diesel fuel for the generators and the generators themselves breaking down.

The installation in the mission houses was a Heath Robinson affair, with cables on the side of the adobe walls supported by insulating blocks. To save cable, the principle that the closest distance between two points is a straight line was followed, so that walls were criss-crossed with different coloured cable leading from light bulbs to switches. No precautions were taken and the system was not earthed.

As we had electricity for limited hours, we sometimes forgot we had it and carried on in the dark or with the paraffin lamp - a useful illustration in my sermons: we have access to spiritual power and light, but fail to be switched on.

21

It takes a long time to grow a bishop

SOME have argued that bishops should be the first people into a pioneering missionary situation, spearheads opening the way with a team and making it possible for ministries to be initiated, rather than a kind of prize for church growth. I think there is a lot to be said for this argument, but evangelism and mission outreach are not always tidy exercises and wisdom often comes with hindsight.

Episcopal oversight was not easy in Argentina: both geographical distance and traditional Anglican styles of leadership made it difficult. This is no way reflects negatively on the bishops that the country has been blessed to have; rather it reflects on the impossible tasks they were expected to do and the areas to cover. At one stage the Bishop at Christ Church Cathedral on the Falkland Islands was responsible for the whole of South America, except for what was then British Honduras (Belize)! Things did gradually become more episcopally manageable, although when I returned in 1963 Bishop Tucker was still titled the Bishop of Argentina, Eastern South America with the Falkland Islands. The beginning of change took place with the appointment of the Revd Kenneth Howell as Bishop of Chile.

The Peter Principle suggests that "everyone rises to the level of his/her inadequacy". I felt that this is what happened when I was consecrated and appointed bishop at the age of 33. Whilst in England on leave I paid my train fare with my Barclaycard and the employee asked me if Bishop was a surname or a title. I rather embarrassingly said it was my title and asked why the question. His reply was, "You look too young". Looking back now, I suppose I should have been pleased.

My appointment was the result of Bishop Tucker's concern to establish a closer and more relevant pastoral relationship with the Indian Church. I remember him saying to me, "My presence is rather like that of a heavenly witchdoctor. I come, I smile, I grunt and lay hands on people, but that is not a pastoral ministry. What I need is someone who speaks the Indian language and Spanish, who has some understanding and sensitivity to the Indian way of thinking and who is preferably Argentine-born. I would, therefore, like you to be an extension of my hands in the north as my Assistant Bishop."

Bishop Tucker's proposition was not to be easily implemented. The presence of new missionaries and the recent arrival and appointment of the Revd Bill Flagg, formerly in Chile and Paraguay, as Field Superintendent and later Archdeacon, brought a new dimension to future strategy. Whilst there was no personal animosity on the part of the missionary team, it was unanimously felt that my appointment as a young bishop over the experienced new archdeacon could have its difficulties. Bishop Tucker was not too happy that his proposal was not immediately welcomed, but was open to discussion to find a way forward.

After further discussions and conferences where the matter was considered and prayed about, it was decided that even more radical changes to the ecclesiastical structures were required.

New diocese

The new proposal was that in the light of geographical distances, the totally different social and ethnic conditions, as well as the completely contrasting cultural backgrounds, plus the fact that the church's work amongst the Indians was developing in a more intensive way, both in the areas of education and other training, it was imperative that leaders with powers of decisions were near at hand. The new pastoral needs and problems required a clearer understanding of the Indian culture and language. The demands and requirements of Northern Argentina were completely different from the needs of Buenos Aires and the south of the country.

It was decided, therefore, to create a new diocese. As far as the Anglican Communion structures were concerned, the diocese in Argentina was still regarded as an Extra-Provincial Diocese of Canterbury, so any changes were subject to the approval of the Archbishop of Canterbury.

Negotiations took place between Bishop Tucker and Canterbury, as well as with the South American Missionary Society and the missionaries in northern Argentina. It had been agreed that if the new plans were to move forward, Archdeacon Bill Flagg should become bishop of the new diocese and I should be consecrated at the same time to serve as his assistant.

I knew that Bishop Tucker would be sad to lose episcopal jurisdiction over the work among the Indians, since it was very close to his heart, but he was the first to realise that such a move was in line with the way the Church was developing and it was important that leadership structures facilitated the ongoing work and growth of the Indian Church.

Following yet more discussions and plans, I received an official letter from Michael Ramsey, Archbishop of Canterbury, inviting me to be consecrated to serve as Assistant Bishop of the Diocese of Northern Argentina and Paraguay. The Archbishop authorised Bishop Tucker, by letters demissary, to consecrate Bill Flagg and me as bishops. Plans were put in hand, all the requirements implemented, and a date fixed for the service in St John's Cathedral, Buenos Aires.

Since the new diocese would still be an Extra-Provincial Diocese of Canterbury, it was required that bishops should make an Oath of Allegiance to the Queen. This was a matter I had not considered and it became for me a real obstacle. In my ministry I had made much of being an Argentine citizen and felt that I had been able to undertake actions and activities on the strength of my Argentine nationality. Yet now here I was, almost on the eve of my consecration, being asked to give allegiance to the Sovereign of a 'foreign power', a matter related to historical factors and the Queen being Head of the Church of England. I expressed my doubts to Bishop Tucker and explained that I did not with all good conscience feel it was right to go forward and that I should withdraw my acceptance.

This caused some consternation, and I remember well the drive I was taken on with Bishop Cyril and others who debated the matter with me. Their argument sounded rather Jesuitical and went along the lines that for ancient historic reasons the Queen was Head of the Church of England, and that my Oath of Allegiance would be in relation to her ecclesiastical function rather than to her standing as head of a foreign state.

The situation was to change very soon, in fact, when the Diocese of Argentina became part of a new Province and ceased to be an Extra-Provincial Diocese under the responsibility of Canterbury. I recognised the wisdom of my senior colleagues and accepted their argument, so all obstacles were removed and plans were set in motion for the consecrations.

My colleagues in Northern Argentina seemed happy with the idea that Bill Flagg would be the new Diocesan Bishop. He was highly respected and a man with experience, not an academic. He was, in fact, a man of the soil, coming from Somerset farming stock. He was full of enthusiasm, and had it not been for the moderating voice and influence of Patrick Harris, he might well have pushed the Church in the north to assume responsibilities and financial commitments it would have been unable to face. It was, however, this enthusiasm which encouraged a positive period in the growth of the Church.

Lands were obtained for the Indians and new buildings erected and the Indian Church turned its vision and evangelism to the Spanish population in the cities of Salta and Formosa, as well as the smaller towns of Ingeniero Juárez and Embarcación. The main thrust of the Church since its early pioneering days was to the marginalised Indians; now it was also to establish a witness to the wider Spanish-speaking people. Although in the strategy of mission such a step seems obvious, there were reservations: some felt it would stretch resources, whilst the Indians felt they had a monopoly of the

Anglican Church.

A certain tension still persists when the minority Spanish-speaking Church and its leaders exert a greater influence in decision making, especially when money matters are in question. The Argentine Church leaders are often paid, whilst the Indian pastors receive no salary. These differences become apparent when attempts are made to hold a united Synod, in which the language used is Spanish. As a result, the Spanish speakers dominate discussions and particularly the older Indians are unable or feel inhibited to make their point of view known. They express themselves more comfortably outside formal sessions over a meal or sitting round the fire at night, which means their views are not taken into consideration, nor included in the formal decision making with its proposers, seconders, debates and votes, a method totally alien to them.

In a sense, there is much to be said for a kind of separate development. Although this may sound like a kind of ecclesiastical apartheid, I think the Indians would be very happy with it and not consider it in any way belittling to them. In towns such as Juárez, the Spanish-speaking settlers worship in Spanish in their churches while the Indians' services are either in Wichi or Toba. There is a certain natural mixing and there are Indians who can express themselves perfectly in Spanish and attend the Spanish services where they are welcomed with no discrimination.

Those were interesting and exciting days, as new structures gradually came into place which served as tools for the development of the Church.

The consecration was arranged to take place at St John's

Cathedral, Buenos Aires, on St Thomas's Day, 21 December 1969. My parents were still in Argentina, so we all travelled to Buenos Aires. Rachel, the children and I stayed as guests at my old school; the boarders were on holiday so there was ample room in the dormitories, and I think my old headmaster, J.E. Vibart, and his wife Chloe were pleased to have us. I think, too, there was a feeling of pride for the school that one of the old boys was to become a bishop!

One felt a sense of history and a following in an apostolic path since the consecration day was exactly 100 years to that of Waite Stirling, the first bishop of the whole of South America (except British Honduras).

Consecration

Bill Flagg and I were duly consecrated by Bishop Tucker, assisted by Bishop Howell of Chile and the recently consecrated Assistant Bishop of Temuco (Chile), Bishop Colin Bazley. But what should have been a memorable spiritual experience and a day to look back on, is sadly just a hazy memory. I do not recall the preacher, the contents of the sermon, the hymns, nor much else of the liturgy and service. But I have no doubt that this was a step and an occasion when it pleased God to call me in a special way for a particular task. This may well be the experience of many on the occasion of their confirmation; but it is not our feelings or memories that count, but the fact that God has acted, God has called, and God has sent. A more meaningful example might be seen in baptism: when we are at our weakest and most vulnerable, God takes us and makes us his children, without us even understanding what is going on.

From now on life was to be different—and yet within the context of my immediate ministry all very much the same.

22

Bishop, Indians and the corridors of power

BACK in Juárez we lived in the same house and took up the same work and ministry, although this obviously broadened. Not only could I baptise and confirm, I could now ordain those called and trained. In a way the Church had come of age, its local ministry no longer having to wait for occasional visits from a bishop who lived far away and who did not speak their language. The Indian churches were truly part of the Anglican Communion infrastructure.

I have always felt it was divine overruling that the Anglican Church was the one that brought the Christian faith to the marginalised Indians, and that the small, isolated communities with their precariously built adobe and brushwood churches were in fact members of the worldwide Anglican family of churches. The episcopal structure means that communities are united under one leader. Had a church with a congregational style of infrastructure been introduced, it could well have divided and isolated the communities. In later years I remember appealing to the Anglican Observer at the United Nations to intercede for the Indians and their land rights. These isolated minorities could make their voice and needs heard at the highest levels immediately.

It took a while for Rachel to get used to being married to a bishop. On one occasion someone came to the house and asked, "Does the bishop live here?" She quickly replied, "No, not here," and then suddenly remembered he did and called them back!

María Irma Torres in her history of Juárez, *Ingeniero Guillermo Nicasio Juárez y los Parajes del Oeste de Formosa,* lists in an appendix local people who had helped provide information for her book, and it is pleasing to see included amongst others in the list: "Jaluf, Salomón (Storeman); Lanoza, Atanacio (Cattleman); Leake, David (Bishop); Loaiza, Zacarías (Cobbler); Ortiz, Miguel (Carpenter)." It was certainly a contrasting style to the princely bishops of history!

There were odd encounters. Patricio Kelly had been head boy at St George's College in Buenos Aires a few years after I was at St Alban's College. He was the son of Bovril's representative in the city of Formosa, and was a qualified doctor with a deep concern for the poor and marginalised. He felt a vocation to politics and had been appointed Minister of Social Welfare in the Province. He quickly looked to me as a kind of kindred spirit and someone with whom he could work. I also felt he was an honest, sensitive man with a deep desire to help the Indians and so we planned together. On his visits to Juárez, he would get the pilot to fly low over our house and dip his wings; I would then drive down in the truck to the airstrip to see him.

Kelly produced projects and budgets that had been put together by so-called experts in Buenos Aires, but they did not fit the reality of Northern Argentina, and even less the idiosyncracies of the Indians. Kelly's argument was that they were the necessary step to get the money we needed. Once we got the money we could adapt the plans to our reality and needs and create work opportunities! These I felt were worthy objectives and so I fell in with his proposals, even though they at first included a poultry project—I pointed out this would be akin to creating a pig farm in a Jewish kibbutz since the Indians didn't eat chickens or eggs.

The only work opportunity was the lumber camps producing *quebracho* posts. At the time there were ample virgin forest areas and I was not as ecologically enlightened as I am today, so did not worry about this intensive deforestation. It horrifies me now, though I suppose if I'd not become involved others would have done so. The Indians were keen to undertake this work and it became the mainstay of the project for a number of years.

It was important to establish a structure within which to undertake the development project. I didn't want to be seen as the *patrón* (boss), and I certainly didn't want the Anglican Church to establish a labour relationship with the Indians to whom we were pastorally responsible, although in many instances this inevitably happened. To establish some economic working structure, we decided to create a cooperative. This seemed the best and 'friendliest' ambience in which to set up and develop a charitable work. We obtained a prototype copy of statutes for the formation of a work cooperative, made adaptations to fit the Indian reality, and presented it to the relevant provincial government department. So the 'Sombrero Negro Cooperative' was formed and officially recognised.

Looking back with the wisdom of hindsight, we might have done things differently. Little did I realise what problems would ensue, but I still think it was right to do it. It was certainly a project that the Indians welcomed and they still look back to the "good old days of the cooperative". It was a kind of 'fat kine' period which was to be followed a few years later by the 'thin kine'.

Keeping accounts was not easy. Bishop Bill Flagg said I had three accounts: personal, diocesan and cooperative, and money corresponding to each was kept in my left pocket, right pocket and back pocket. He said that as Indians, storemen or post seller were paid, the appropriate pocket was dipped into. There was an element of truth in this!

Patricio Kelly was pleased I was heading up the project and, as well as helping with government funding and giving moral support, he took a keen interest in all that was being done. It was a period of ferment, change and uncertainty in Argentina. Radical elements were challenging the military government. All was well provided you were feeding hungry Indians; asking why they were hungry elicited a different response.

Kelly delegated two young brothers to come and work with us, typical hirsute radicals from Buenos Aires. One took an inordinate interest in our shelves of books, presumably to see where we stood in our social motivation. They became part of the cooperative staff, mobilising and infiltrating the Indian communities with radical ideas.

They caused some of my biggest headaches. They regularly ordered lorryloads of basic foodstuffs, flour, maize, sugar and *yerba*, from the stores in Juárez and Morillo to be freely distributed amongst the village Indians along the Pilcomayo. The stores were happy to comply with the orders, confident they would be paid as I was head of the cooperative. But the storemen started to arrive on my doorstep with handfuls of unpaid bills. These storemen were themselves unscrupulous people who had undoubtedly made a lot of money in dishonest ways and underhand dealing, as well as using the Indians over many years for what would almost amount to slave labour. The two brothers argued that what was being given to the Indians was their due in the light of all the persecution they had suffered at the hands of these oppressors. I felt a certain sympathy with their reasoning, but it was a position certainly not accepted by the storemen!

I got to a stage of dreading the regular visits of Atta Gerala from Morillo in his distinctive orange-painted lorry. A pot-bellied Arab who had become very wealthy, his appearance belied his riches. He would arrive dressed in a grubby tee-shirt and light pyjama trousers held up by a cord, shuffling along in slippers and waving a wad of bills in his hand. I attended him as graciously as I could, mumbled vague comments about "*Mañana, mañana*" and went back into the house praying for wisdom, awaiting a further visit when I would give the same reply.

In due course the position became untenable, so I went to the city of Formosa to engage a lawyer. I explained the situation clearly to him. He outlined a wordy document which in essence absolved me from any responsibility for orders I had not formally made and signed for, and established that I could not be held responsible for the actions of individuals within the cooperative. I returned to Juárez and made it known to the storemen that I would pay all the bills if they would present the orders duly signed with my signature as Director of the Cooperative. No signed orders could be produced and so no bills were paid. From then on, the storemen were careful not to provide any merchandise without my authority; while it had lasted the Indians enjoyed the benefits.

I'm sure that none of the stores lost out when I consider the many years of dishonest dealings. The Arab businessmen maintained a friendly relationship in the knowledge that in due course they would get some further opportunity to defraud. They had lost a battle, but not the war. Even after retirement, when I returned to visit Northern Argentina and crossed with Gerala's orange-coloured lorry on highway 81, I felt my old anxiety return.

The cooperative was valued by the Indians, who felt they were helped and treated fairly. It meant work opportunity and brought more finances into the town. For me, it was not always easy since I was seen one moment as the bishop with pastoral concerns and next as the employer who on occasions had to discipline or dismiss people or was accused of not making payments.

With government changes and a drying-up of subsidies from central government, the project was wound down and I was called to present all the accounts to the Ministry of Social Welfare. I travelled to Formosa with files full of facts and figures and multiple copies of receipts. The lady who attended me was rather officious and, on examining the project and the accounts, noted that some money had been spent in areas not projected for. I pointed out that the Minister, Dr Patricio Kelly, had told me to get on and "create work opportunities". She replied that that was all very well, but the minister had now resigned and it was her responsibility to receive my account statement and present it to the Provincial Accounts Tribunal who, she said, would question the presentation—besides which, each receipt had to be presented in triplicate!

I stuck to my guns, arguing the case, and then suggested to her that I might go and see the President of the Accounts Tribunal to talk the matter through with him. I collected my papers, had all my receipts copied, and where this was not possible obtained receipt dockets from a service station, and then argued my case with the President of the Accounts Tribunal over a cup of coffee, recounting to him the story of how the project had been presented and carried out, admitting that whilst all the money had not been spent exactly on what the project had envisaged, I had done my best and my report and receipts reflected a true picture of our endeavours to help the Indians.

He was convinced by my argument and promised he would have no problem in accepting the presentation via the Ministry of Social Welfare. I returned much relieved to Government House and presented my files to the accountant who gave me a signed and rubber-stamped letter of acceptance and the ordeal was closed.

Hunting and gathering in the corridors of power

The early groundwork undertaken by the missionaries in the education field was proving its worth. The new generation of Indians was now able to take advantage of primary education. With this basic knowledge and experience, new work opportunities opened to them and many were quick to take them. There was a kind of adaptation of their natural hunting and gathering tradition to the new reality: not now stalking game in the forest, but politicians and civil servants in the corridors of government house.

With their greater fluency in Spanish, they were able to make their needs known. Their fathers had spoken a kind of Tarzan Spanish, talking about "I eating yesterday" and "Me wanting buying flour". In Toba you don't conjugate verbs as in Spanish with a present, past and future.

The first work opportunities were as nursing orderlies in their villages or in some cases in the town hospitals. These posts were filled by men since they were the ones who had taken the opportunity to study. They proved themselves, and were soon able to give injections, take blood pressure and administer TB treatment. An interesting spin-off was that the Argentine settlers also went to them for treatment. A nursing orderly in a village would probably be the only wage-earner and would feed the whole of the village, who might well be mostly his extended family. The first orderlies were supervised by the Director of the Juárez hospital, who in turn delegated this responsibility to one of the missionary nurses.

Indians with at least sixth grade were appointed as assistant teachers, working in the state school established on each mission station. Their job description was to be bilingual teachers, which in practice meant that they were present to interpret and translate for the Spanish-speaking teacher and help the children understand what was being taught.

A further unseen development was that patients were less reticent about going as long-term in-patients for TB treatment in the cities of Salta or Formosa. Many of these patients quietly and imperceptibly learnt or improved their Spanish, became acquainted with the routine of hospital life and made friends with Argentine patients. They unwittingly applied their traditional instincts in making acquaintance with hospital staff, who were drawn to help them materially. Their presence in the hospitals had the further effect of highlighting the Indian reality to the medical staff, many of whom had never ventured beyond the limits of their own cities.

When the patients returned home, they often took with them clothes given by benefactors, and also a broader outlook on life. In their villages they became key people, influential orientators and interpreters, helping their people understand the new enveloping Argentine culture, as well as interpreting the Indian culture and customs to Argentine visitors and government officials.

A new development was a fashionable interest in ethnic and related Indian matters. This was reflected in the government creating special departments to look after Indian affairs. Undoubtedly the creation of such specialised departments was encouraged by those who saw the possibilities of further posts and incomes with little work.

The Indians were not slow in seeking posts and being offered, maybe as tokenism, some minor responsibilities. They took as models their Argentine overlords, and such phrases as *Tengo un puesto* (I have a post) or *Me llegó el nombramiento* (My appointment has been confirmed) were synonymous with lazing around and doing nothing!

I recall going to the *Instituto Comunitario Aborigen* office in Juárez, and the person behind the desk noticed that a Government inspector was approaching. He whispered to the Indian standing not far from me, "Get the broom and look as if you're doing something." The Indian's reply was that he had worked six years to get the job and he was not going to do any more work now! This reminded me of the occasion when I was sweeping outside our house—I have always found sweeping a floor to be very therapeutic: it gives quick and obvious results for little effort. An approaching Indian said to me, "Oh you're working." I replied that I was not in fact working as I enjoyed what I was doing. I asked him for his definition of work and after some thought he replied: "Work is what you've done when you're tired after you've done it".

23

Seeing life at the sharp end

RACHEL undertook Andrew's and Philip's initial teaching in English. Since all their games took place outside, it was a great achievement even to get them quiet and sitting down, and then no sooner was this accomplished than some caller would arrive, Rachel would be distracted, attend the caller, and the boys meanwhile would often escape. Later they were to benefit, as did Judith, from dedicated teachers Robert Day and Robyn Langford.

Although they grew up amidst many potential dangers, providentially they were kept safe. Knives and machetes were their early toys, and on one occasion Philip, whilst playing with his friend Fernando, the young son of a near neighbour, had a potentially serious accident. Fernando decided he had finished the game and threw his machete into the air in Philip's direction, catching him at the back of the skull and cutting a two-inch gash in his scalp. We rushed him down to the hospital where Dr Toribio Aranda stitched it up and Philip soon recovered, although he retains a clear scar.

Only in later years did I hear that one of the boys' regular games was to follow and attempt to hang on to the slow-moving cargo train when it passed not far from our house. Snakes were a constant fear. Our bathroom had leaky drains and the damp adobes were a happy home for frogs which attracted the snakes. I remember once seeing the intertwined tails of two snakes hanging over the edge of the adobe wall-support of the bath. On another occasion Rachel in desperation flung her wooden Schol sandal at a coral snake, killing it instantly by a well aimed hit on the head! There are many other instances of close encounters with snakes, centipedes and scorpions.

During our time in Formosa, our daughter Judith was bitten on her toe by a small piranha whilst bathing in the river and was rescued from the shallow water by Andrew. He narrowly escaped a more serious accident when he ran into the sharp corner of a low overhanging zinc roof panel on a building in Misión San Patricio, escaping with a scar at the side of his nose. We thank God for His protection from danger because medical help was often not available.

As my mother used to say: "We don't have much money, but we do see life". This saying has remained with the children and grandchildren. Life in Northern Argentina amongst the Indians was an enriching experience, always full of the unexpected, a life in a climatically hostile environment, a continual struggle for many to gain a livelihood, witnessing and living the reality of conflicting cultures and values, involved in the suffering of the oppressed, advocating on their behalf with hostile oppressors. Such a lifestyle stood in stark contrast to the occasional intervals taken for 'home leave', which meant a journey to England by sea and later by air, a time to visit loved ones and friends and renew links with people and churches whose giving, prayers and shared concern for the spread of the gospel of Jesus Christ made it possible for the life and work we were involved in to take place.

I remember as a child boarding the ship *Empire Deben* in Buenos Aires en route for Southampton and being astonished to hear the white steward who carried our case to the cabin speak in English. All those I had met who did such work had been dark-skinned and certainly did not speak English. To be served by an English waiter at table was another eye-opener. In later years, to travel to Buenos Aires from the north by air, cutting a five-day journey to three hours, was extraordinary. To stay in a comfortable hotel with electric light and air-conditioning contrasted vividly with nights in Indian villages with the stars and moon as a ceiling, the oppressive heat under a mosquito net and the cicadas' unabated screeching. Life was a rich and colourful mosaic of different extremes. Certainly not much money, but we did see life!

It was while we were on leave in England that Judith was born just before Christmas 1967. We were living with Rachel's parents in Cromer in a terraced house with no less than 21 rooms including bathrooms. It had no central heating and in the winter was very cold. Apart from the warmth in the kitchen, the only permanent heating was an open wood or coal fire in Mr Yarham's study, where his table in the middle of the room was surrounded by books and papers which seemed gradually to encroach upon his desk space, often leaving little room for the extended logs he had on the fire!

Besides his responsibilities as headmaster of the village school of Roughton, he devoted much time to freelance journalism. He had a personalised system of filing his paper cuttings. He would read the local and national newspaper every day, as well as any other magazines he could get his hands on, marking any matter of interest, and cutting these bits of information out and filing them in shoeboxes scattered on the floors of the many rooms in the house. He was an endless source of information on all subjects, and with his paper cuttings as a valuable resource would as easily write about "Weather Stations in the Antarctic" as "Farming Down the Ages".

Judith's birth at a maternity home in West Runton completed our family and rejoiced both parents and brothers! A few months later we would return to Argentina where Judith was to grow up and become friends with the little Wichi children who arrived in Misión Chaqueña with their parents who were attending the Bible School. At an early age she acquired the Wichi language, as well as adapting to their games and ways of playing. She accompanied these children to school and when bored would often return home with them.

All Change

The cooperative development project in due course came to an end. While it lasted many Indians benefited, but like most projects it left little long-term benefit. Many had food and it served as a further experience along the road for the Indians as they sought to adapt and change and become part of the solution to their many problems. Generally speaking, they would look back on all such experiences positively and when things went wrong on some future occasion would comment, "It was not like this when Don David was responsible"—which is rather pleasing even if untrue, since when I was responsible many things certainly did go wrong! I valued the experience of directing the cooperative, but was not sorry to be relieved of the responsibility.

Pastoral involvement with the Indians was interesting and

exciting. There was little routine and certainly no established pattern; you had to meet the needs as they surfaced. Many Indians from the Pilcomayo and the Bermejo river villages were moving away from their traditional homelands and establishing themselves on the outskirts of Juárez and other towns along the railway line. Those from the Pilcomayo were being driven away partly because the river was gradually silting up its main course and tributaries were flowing north into Paraguay or south, leaving them with areas which became unpredictable flood plains. A large number of Wichi from the original Misión San Andrés and the other outlying missions moved out of the flood area and established a new centre in El Potrillo, about 80 kilometres from Juárez. There they maintained their traditional village and family identities, with each group establishing its community and settling in an identifiable location. Although they were all fairly close together, each group retained its leaders and pastors and built its own church, thus creating a number of churches in a relatively small area.

The exodus from homelands was a further blow to the Indians' natural traditional subsistence lifestyle, making them more dependent on outsiders' help and thus influence. El Potrillo became an attraction for many well-intentioned 'do-gooders'; though still in the forest, it was accessible to Juárez and, being a 'new town' located away from the original Anglican areas of influence, different churches and agencies felt it was 'up for grabs'.

The Roman Catholic Church developed a strong presence and nuns took on nursing and teaching posts, whilst evangelical churches in Buenos Aires, often lacking anthropological sensitivity and with little understanding of history or missiology, would arrive with lorry loads of used clothing and free out-of-date medical samples, hoping to ingratiate themselves with the Indians. The Indians would often take advantage of the immediate benefits, but their loyalty to the Anglican Church remained constant. They were true to the motif, “grab all that comes from above unless it’s lightning!”

In our work we had to accept the reality of not being able to plan long-term. Travelling was unpredictable, with the rains often making it impossible to get petrol. The Indians’ leaving riverside villages to live in town brought them into many new and unpredictable situations: how to acquire an identity document, get children into school, obtain medical attention, induce the boss to pay them a long overdue wage, face the police or the local JP in an unfair decision. In the course of a day, one faced these and multiple and varied problems, but in the end all one could do was be available and accessible to those with problems. I would often stand or sit not far from our house and the people and their needs arrived on their own. I rationalised this style of service and termed it the ‘ministry of availability’, acting as a sounding board as people moved from one lifestyle to another.

I certainly could not think in terms of working from an office with fixed hours. Some would criticise this way as pandering to the Indians, but it was a style they readily understood and accepted, it met them at their point of need, and I think in great measure fitted into their style of sharing. I did find it important for the Indians to realise that I did not have the monopoly of a solution, any more than they had the monopoly of the problem. It was important that they should gradually realise they had a part to play in finding solutions. I might be able to find money to cover the cost of medicine, but they had to make the effort and understand the logistics of getting to see the doctor and obtaining the prescription. Gradually these kinds of problems got sorted out and the Indian patients began to manage the system.

I often reached the end of the day exhausted and not having been able to provide a full solution to any of the problems. In fact, all I could expect was to have had the privilege of sharing part of the long pilgrimage, endeavouring to walk in their *alpargatas* (simple sandals) for a few miles, and hopefully helped to level the often painful road.

The process of 'accompaniment' was not without its amusing and tragicomic experiences. Once having helped a man get to hospital early one morning, I encountered him later looking relieved and better. When I asked him how things had gone, he replied positively, thinking that merely having the prescription in his shirt pocket would help with his heart condition. On another occasion, a man in great pain told me he had been chewing a page from John's Gospel all day but still had toothache! It was not uncommon to see a TB patient lying with a Mark's Gospel on his chest. It was inevitable in a transcultural sharing of the Christian gospel that such syncretistic expressions would be encountered.

I was also involved in helping the Indians obtain their identity documents, which meant much time taking photographs (for which I was paid with fish) followed by early hours in the registry office. This procedure was later accelerated and done 'once for all' by the military who sent a team of photographers, secretaries and other personnel in army trucks to document en masse in all the villages. In recognition of my endeavours I was invited by the officer in charge to present the first documents. The obtaining of such meant that the Indians were no longer regarded as foreigners in their own country but as full Argentine citizens, with the right to vote and also the responsibility of being drafted into compulsory military service. This process in Argentina was allocated by a kind of lottery in which the last three numbers of your identity card determined whether you were to serve in the army, navy or air force. Conscription has since been abolished.

Navarrete from the Wichi community in Juárez was called up to the navy, spending his time in Puerto Belgrano in the Province of Buenos Aires. On his return during leave, he cut an impressive figure in the summer version of his naval uniform. Regrettably, though, he became involved in a bout of drinking which was to cost him his life. Pure alcohol is available in most of the stores and the practice was to dilute it with a small amount of water. After adding some water to his bottle, he bent over the tap to take a drink when his drinking companion hit him over the head with a heavy piece of wood and killed him. Renguito was suspected and arrested. He was from the village on the opposite side of the makeshift airstrip commonly referred to as "Frans' Mission". Frans was a Norwegian Pentecostal missionary whose followers were a breakaway group of Wichi who maintained an ongoing feud with the Anglicans living on the opposite side of the strip.

Rosendo Navarrete, the dead man's father, became mentally perturbed about the whole affair and feared for his own life because of the accusation against Renguito, so I arranged for him to stay with us at the Anglican centre.

The whole affair became complex, with accusations and counter-accusations, during which I was questioned and interrogated and had to travel to see the judicial authorities in Formosa. At one stage, the judge authorised that the body be exhumed for further forensic investigation. This event in the cemetery was witnessed by a great crowd of onlookers. The forensic medical officer in his white overall and rubber gloves took the skull and washed dirt and loose bits away. He displayed it for all to see the bone damage and fractures just above the right ear where the murderer had clubbed his victim. The evidence was clarified, and Renguito was imprisoned.

The Navarrete affair was one of the most tragic events during our time in Juárez, but we were often involved in similar, if less dramatic, events relating to the Indians. Formerly, their differences, even when deaths were involved, were sorted out either by revenge or some payment under the traditional ethnic customs and taboos. It is worthy of mention that when an inter-tribal revenge death occurred in the early days of Misión San Andrés, the response of those involved was not to instigate further revenge and murder, but to send a group of leaders to share the gospel with the murderers, an instance of the Christian message of peace and forgiveness really taking root.

Liberation theology was much in vogue at this time. It focused on the need to identify with one's social environment and to help people towards an awareness of the political and social implications of their situation. Much was spoken and written about the exploiters and the exploited. Certainly liberation theology borrowed from dialectical materialism, and it found in the Indian situation fertile ground and textbook cases for its application. The good news of the liberationists, however, was more related to the message of Exodus than to the gospel of the New Testament.

There were many areas of liberation theology that appealed to our sensitive social conscience and we were happy to borrow from this discipline, but we soon became aware of its limitations and its potential to move from peaceful acts of civil disobedience to violence, and areas of involvement which really were not the road the Indians would want to take. We have always been humbled by their longsuffering and acceptance of unjust situations. The danger of many 'liberation theorists' was to use the 'Indian problem' as a field in which to develop their pet theologies and theories.

My option and dedication to the poor were motivated rather by a commitment to Jesus Christ and an expression of His love in fulfilment of the apostle Paul's admonition that "whilst we have opportunity let us do good, especially to them who are of the household of faith", together with Jesus' claim that He had come to the world to give life in all its abundance. This was starkly not the case while children died from basic diseases and malnutrition, while they were not accepted in schools or the sick into hospitals, while people had not full rights as Argentine citizens and no rights to their ancestral lands, and were exploited by unscrupulous employers.

Judith with two friends

24

The Malvinas/Falklands conflict

WHEN people know that I come from Argentina, the conversation inevitably turns to the South Atlantic conflict of 1982. The nearest I have been to the Falkland Islands, or the *Islas Malvinas* as they are known in Argentina, was a visit I arranged through the generosity and kindness of the Argentine Navy for myself and other church leaders to *Bahía Aguirre* (Spaniard Harbour) to the cave where the founder of the South American Missionary Society, Captain Allen Gardiner R.N., died in 1851.

The year 1982 remains a watershed year. The mobilisation of the populace to the Plaza de Mayo in the centre of Buenos Aires on 29 March to demonstrate against the *de facto* government was quickly thwarted by the President, General Galtieri, and held back by heavy-handed police action. Yet the same people were encouraged to throng the same square on 2 April to hear Galtieri announce that the Argentine Army had landed on the Malvinas.

The islands have been in contention since the early history of the Argentine Republic and have always presented an evocative, external, focal point of unity when there has been internal dissension. Once the government is threatened by discord within its borders, an appeal to the sovereignty of the islands is sure to unite the populace. Official highway signs as well as graffiti clearly announce LAS MALVINAS SON ARGENTINAS. As Anglo-Argentine children, we were brought up very conscious of this contention and Argentine sovereignty was clearly supported. One satirist at school

Graffiti (Malvinas Argentinas) on Lambeth Palace wall across from the Houses of Parliament

made the Solomonic suggestion that they should be Argentine in the morning when we did our lessons in Spanish and British in the afternoons when we did English lessons!

I had been appointed Bishop of Northern Argentina in 1979 in succession to Bishop Patrick Harris, who had succeeded Bishop Bill Flagg in 1973. Pat thought it providential that as an Argentine citizen I should have been in place prior to the 1982 war as it meant that the bishop was an Argentine-born national. We had moved to live in the city of Salta, where the offices of the diocese are situated.

The conflict gave rise to the most outrageous and outlandish rumours, with perhaps the most colourful being that with the inhabitants of British descent in the islands and the Anglican diocese in the north of Argentina, a pincer movement was planned from extreme south to extreme north to take over the whole country!

Soon after the announcement of the Argentine landings, I received an anonymous letter with this strangely worded message, translated from Spanish:

The English Heretic once again attacks St Peter.

1532. England separates itself from Rome, in this way consummating its first attack on the Church of St Peter.

1982. 450 years later "England" again attacks St Peter (South Georgia), not acceding to the endeavours of the church's inheritor Pope John Paul II, who at the request of his sons in Argentina and Chile extended his pacific mediation to the southern seas.

Out with the perfidious Anglican from the unredeemed South America.

Out with the Mason or die here.

(signed) Gaucho Rivero Commando Group

This was followed by a letter telling us that we would be blown up. I said nothing to Rachel, but later in the day she answered a clandestine phone message nervously fixing the time of the attack. I had to explain to her that I had received these threats and that this call was the follow-up. In the light of the tragic period of the Dirty War when an estimated 30,000 people were blown up or disappeared, we could not ignore the threat, especially as such actions were often preceded by anonymous warnings.

Where does a bishop go when he's in trouble? I found an archbishop: I went to see Monseñor Mariano Pérez, the Roman Catholic Archbishop of Salta. He was in his chapel for his evening prayers, and when he finished he kindly met me in his office and listened to my predicament. He said it was a coincidence that his Bible reading was the persecution of Paul and Barnabas in Lystra and the imprisonment of Paul and Silas in Philippi. He then added, "Well, the lot of leadership in the Church is that we shall be vulnerable to persecution." However right he was, this did not exactly comfort me! Maybe if like him I had been celibate I could have coped, but I had a wife and three children.

I opted for some practical help and saw a lawyer friend, Héctor Yarade, who had himself been *persona non grata* with the military governments. His advice was not to sleep in the same bed for two consecutive nights, and he offered me there and then to stay at his house for the night. I returned home to Rachel and the family and we opted to stay at the home of our friend and colleague, Helena Oliver, in Cerrillos on the outskirts of Salta. During the Dirty War, I had been instrumental in helping Helena get out of Argentina when she was threatened, and she had had to spend some time in England and later in Somalia until it was safe to return. Bishop Harris had also helped Helena's brother-in-law, Enrique Pfister, who had been Provincial Minister of Finance, to go into exile in Venezuela. He was the only minister in the Salta government not to be assassinated or dropped from a plane into a large reservoir, as was the suspected fate of the Governor at the time, Dr Raggone.

With Helena Oliver (Wallis) and Bishop Mario

In the end, we spent only one night away from our home. We remained there rather nervously at first and then got used to the tension and uncertainty. I took the precaution of taking the letter to the police, who decided to place a guard on our home for three months. A dark, dirty mark from his blue uniform was left in the corner of our veranda where he dropped off to sleep every night. Rachel prepared a flask and biscuits before we went to bed and placed them on the windowsill for him. He accepted the seat in the truck parked in the road until he was found asleep by his officers as they went on their rounds and reprimanded.

Rachel and I felt our responsibility was to remain at our post.

There was much uncertainty in the north of Argentina with regard to the war and the safety of British missionaries. Unlike Buenos Aires, a cosmopolitan city with many fair-haired Europeans, the *gringos* in Salta and Formosa stood out like sore thumbs. Mothers were concerned for their children and as bishop I felt a special responsibility for them, so it was decided that the expatriate missionaries should be temporarily exiled in Asunción. Bishop Douglas Milmine and his colleagues in Paraguay were kind and hospitable and the families and some single ladies joined in the exodus.

Generous and kind support

Apart from the threat from the Gaucho Rivero Commando Group, we received nothing but generous and kind support from friends and strangers. Rachel was always sensitive about being British and would say she was from Europe! One day when she was out shopping, a lady noted her English accent, gave her a bear hug and said, "No, my dear, don't worry; it's not your fault." One could not think of anyone less likely to cause a conflict!

The evacuation of expatriate missionaries to Paraguay was not without its undercover element, particularly in the case of Dick and Jen Hines who were living in remote Misión La Paz by the River Pilcomayo on the border with Paraguay. It was thought that rather than travel all the way to Salta, it would be best if they crossed the river at La Paz and then find their way to Asunción by whatever means possible. The Paraguayan authorities were helpful and they made their journey that way, leaving most of their belongings in La Paz. This action probably attracted some adverse attention from the Gendarmería Nacional, but nothing was ever said, nor was the action questioned.

Joyce Illingworth from Yorkshire, who speaks Spanish indistinguishably from a native Argentine and could easily be taken for a Latin, firmly decided she was not going to Paraguay and remained in Salta with us for the period of the conflict, before later moving to work in Buenos Aires.

What we had anticipated would be a conflict of two or three weeks stretched into three months, and some of the missionaries were relocated, others returned to Britain, whilst others eventually returned to Argentina.

When Beryl Gilbert returned to her mud-brick house in the Wichi village in Juárez and re-encountered all her kitchen-ware and battered saucepans, exclaimed, “Oh, it’s like Christmas all over again!”

The war coincided with the football World Cup and we had been lent a black and white TV, so this provided some diversion as well as the opportunity of inviting the police guard to come in and watch with us. The programmes were regularly interrupted with martial music and official reports by the military junta. Our more reliable news came over the radio from Montevideo or the BBC World Service.

Terrible cost and awful aftermath

One of the first soldiers to die on the Malvinas was a young conscript from Salta named Guanca. The arrival of his body was orchestrated to create a high profile occasion and no less than 500 cars accompanied his coffin from the airport. Sadly, the many deaths that followed could not be given such great honour and many were buried on the islands. Since the war, arrangements have been made for next of kin to visit the graves of their loved ones, buried in the frozen peat thousands of miles away from their familiar sub-tropical surroundings, many of them having come from northern Argentina.

The conflict finally ended with the signing of surrender treaties, although it was never formally declared a war. Tragic stories are told of the lack of care and provision made by the Argentine authorities for their demobilised troops, who in many cases, it is said, had to find their own way home; many ended in psychiatric institutions and a high percentage committed suicide. More than 20 years on, ex-combatants still walk the suburban trains of Buenos Aires in military camouflage giving out stickers of the Argentine flag and collecting donations. Although their initial spiel is an unequivocal criticism of the military and the current government for not giving due care and adequate pensions to ex-combatants, I always felt a little uncomfortable as they passed down the carriage if I were reading the English-language *Buenos Aires Herald.*

For a number of years the Argentine and British governments had no diplomatic relations. I still have a British passport from the Swiss Embassy who cared for British interests; it was issued in the same building but with a different name and flag over the front door. Statements and expressions of anger and breakdown in relationships were expressed and streets renamed *Islas Malvinas*. Even in my old school, the library was designated the Islas Malvinas Library, but the big change was that Plaza Británica outside Retiro railway station was renamed Plaza *Fuerza Aérea* (Air Force Plaza). Nevertheless, the British coat of arms still adorns one side of the clock tower and when it is working the clock still sounds the time with the Westminster chimes. With the passing of the years, the former name is often in current use.

With the military government's credibility gone, democracy restored, and the need to rebuild commercial links, steps were gradually taken to re-establish lines of communication with Britain. Matters had reached a low ebb and Britain maintained only a skeleton staff under a *chargé d'affaires* at the Swiss Embassy, but just as many thought it was a case of closing shop, relations began to be rebuilt and by April 1990 all was set for the exchange of ambassadors.

To Westminster Abbey and a call to reconciliation

Then occurred something I never dreamed could happen. I received an invitation from the Dean and Chapter of Westminster Abbey and the London-based South Atlantic Council to preach in the abbey at a Thanksgiving Service to mark the re-establishment of formal relations between Argentina and Britain.

My mind went back to my birthplace in Sombrero Negro and the church built with cane and its congregation of Toba Indians, mothers suckling their babies, with chickens scratching and dogs fighting, an illiterate but faithful Indian evangelist wiping the sweat from his brow as he preached his sermon—such a world apart from Westminster Abbey! I thought of the richness and breadth of the Anglican Communion, and wondered at this unexpected and special honour.

I set about preparing the sermon, which I was told by the Dean was to be no longer than 13 minutes. We were now living in Buenos Aires and I was fortunate to have people willing to undertake research for me. It was probably one of my shortest sermons, which took longest to prepare. I don't recall who covered my fare—it may have been courtesy of British Airways, who gave me a Business Class seat. A long flight for 13 minutes!

I duly arrived at the abbey and from my seat in the choir stalls I could see only a sparse congregation. It was not until the beadle led me to the pulpit and I had a full view of the transepts that I was able to appreciate a large gathering and recognise many people with Argentine connections, including the Argentine *chargé d'affaires* in Britain and Lord Montgomery, the son of Viscount Montgomery, who took a keen interest in Anglo-Argentine matters. It was a particular joy to see friends from Buenos Aires.

I said the prayer of invocation in Spanish: "*En el Nombre del Padre, del Hijo y del Espíritu Santo…*" I heard later that this rather startled some who thought that the whole sermon would be in Spanish, but I felt it served to make a statement. I continued in English, and the sermon can be read in Appendix 2.

After the service it was a moving experience to meet many people with Argentine connections, as well as others concerned for Anglo-Argentine relations. Together with my son Philip and daughter-in-law Victoria and a niece, we were entertained to tea in the Deanery.

25

God's other plans: an unexpected move to the capital

OVER the years the work of the Church in the north became consolidated. The ordained Indian priests, well trained at the Bible Institute in Misión Chaqueña, established their role and ministry, whilst Bishop Mario Mariño did the same in his capacity. Missiologists would have been happy with the developments. The establishment of ordained leadership in the Church was admired by our Roman Catholic friends, who accepted the fact that it would be unlikely for them to do the same as long as their Church retained a celibate priesthood.

We had the joy and privilege of witnessing and being part of a Church that had come of age. To visit a church and assist at a confirmation was a moving occasion, as the local pastor in his white poncho-style vestment with a black stripe over the shoulders would assist Bishop Mario in his white poncho with red stripes. These simple robes gave a true semblance of Anglican worship, were easy to make and to keep clean, and in some way reflected the traditional poncho so common in Argentina.

Our children were entering new experiences. By 1989 Andrew had completed his university degrees and was married to María, Philip was in the UK having completed his course at the Royal Agricultural College in Cirencester, followed by a course in mental health nursing in Norwich, and Judith was completing her studies at Dorset House School of Occupational Therapy in Oxford.

Prayers before Confirmation service in Lomas de Zamora

Looking back, I suppose it was an opportune moment for a change in ministry, although at the time we had not contemplated leaving the Indians; I felt this was my role for life, it was my home, it was where I was born, the Tobas were my first friends, their language my first language, and I never felt happier than when driving along the rough, muddy or dusty tracks of the Chaco making pastoral visits to the Indian villages. I enjoyed the challenge of polemical exchanges with government officials as I sought to acquire Indians their rights; I loved advocacy work in police stations and courts, and visiting the sick in hospital.

Rachel had been taken fully into the Indians' hearts. If I

arrived at a village without her, I was reprimanded. The first question would be, "Where is Raquel?" Although medical care was now fully covered by the missionary nurses as well as the government hospital services, Rachel was still looked to for medicines when out in the villages. She was also the one to whom people would make multiple requests and with whom women would share their problems. She was sometimes overwhelmed by the people and being of a sensitive nature did not always find visits easy.

The joys and sorrows were all part of a happy, colourful mosaic of life in a part of the world that was home, where we knew almost everyone and everyone knew us. We were where we wanted to be, happy and fulfilled.

Unexpected letter

Every time we took off from Aeroparque in Buenos Aires to fly back to Salta, Rachel would look out of the window on the sprawling city and the northern suburbs of Gran Buenos Aires and comment: "Thank God we don't have to live there." I echoed her sentiments, although we were soon to see that God had other plans. In 1989 I received a formal letter from Buenos Aires inviting me to allow my name to be nominated as candidate to become Bishop of Argentina in succession to Richard Cutts, whose retirement was imminent. I mused and prayed over the matter, my natural human reaction being to say no, bearing in mind our feelings for the Indians.

As days passed and the deadline became close, I chose to delegate the decision to God! I filled in the forms and sent them off right on the deadline; in fact, I think they had to be collected from the airport to comply with the date for their return. I reflected that it was not my whim that had to be done, but God's will. I prayed He would direct the outcome, with which I would be happy to comply.

The election date was fixed for a day in June 1989 at the cathedral; there were five candidates, the other four being clergy already serving in the diocese. The diocesan electoral system is that the Diocesan Council becomes the Electoral College and votes for the new bishop, the voters being divided into the House of Clergy and House of Laity. The successful candidate has to muster a two-thirds majority, with the candidate gaining the least number of votes dropping out and further ballots being held until that majority is achieved. In the first ballot I was accorded the necessary two-thirds from the laity, and a majority but short of the two-thirds by the clergy, so a further ballot was held. This time I achieved the majority required in both houses, and so it was announced that I was the new bishop-elect of the Diocese of Argentina.

I quickly left the impressive cathedral and the hubbub of the electors to discuss the result and take my return flight to Salta. I departed with a heavy heart as I mused on having to leave the north, to exchange responsibility for the many Indian communities, the long truck journeys on earth tracks often turned to sand or mud, the smoky Indian fires and the smell of cooking fish, for the bustle of a metropolis, commuting by bus and underground, social events at the English Club, church fetes and 'old boys' lunches. I had to remember that I had sent in the forms accepting the nomination and leaving the outcome to God, and must now take the result as His purpose

Cathedral of St John the Baptist, Buenos Aires

for the next stage of our lives. I sensed a feeling of excitement, with new horizons and opportunities.

As a priest, I once reflected that my business was 'God and people'. God is everywhere and there are people everywhere, so I would not be out of a job! As a boy, I had lived in the southern suburbs of Buenos Aires as a school boarder for nine years so the city was not unfamiliar, and although almost 40 years had passed I would have the opportunity of renewing some old friendships.

Back in Salta, Rachel had been informed of the election result. We talked and prayed matters through, and realised that this was the first time in our lives that we moved with reluctance. But a gradual sense of excitement at something new and different drove us forward as we said our goodbyes and packed our belongings.

We were treated to a stormy departure from Salta, with lightning and heavy rain, and made for Rosario de la Frontera, staying the night at the Hotel Termas where we had enjoyed happy holidays with the children. Refreshed, we continued south towards Buenos Aires, our old Dodge 1500 behaving well, and we had no mishaps or delays on the near 1000-mile journey. The nearer we got to Buenos Aires the greater the traffic, but this gradual process acclimatised me to a new style of driving and once we reached General Paz Avenue and dropped down Calle Ugarte into the leafy suburb of Olivos I was quite relaxed.

We turned into Calle Rioja to see Lavaque's large removals van with all our worldly goods climbing the pavement outside No. 2995 and bringing down the telephone lines! The coca-chewing Salta removal men soon had all our belongings and furniture stowed in the bishop's 'palace' which would be our happy home and guesthouse for the next 12 years.

John Woolcock and Derek Chennel were the doyens of the remaining British community in the Anglican church in Buenos Aires, and made it their responsibility to ensure we were happily settled in our home and environment. John was to be a great help in the first few years as a friend and also as Diocesan Treasurer. I'm sure there were times when he must have become frustrated with my procrastination and lack of clear directives, but he was patient, spent time evaluating situations, and did not pull his punches when he thought I ought to take certain action. He had no hesitation in telling me if I made mistakes. I'm sure he saved me from many pitfalls, especially in matters related to finance.

Derek Chennel was endued with an unmanageable sense of humour and approached even serious situations from a cheerful perspective. He was a great help in our first few weeks, as we had to prepare the house for the pre-arranged visit of the Archbishop of Canterbury, his wife, secretary and chaplains. The imminent arrival of these important visitors was a great incentive to the diocese to get new curtains, repair furniture, and above all to put wooden support slats under the slack bedsprings. Lambeth Palace sent out Canon Roger Symon, Archbishop's Chaplain for Anglican Affairs, to reconnoitre and Rachel was embarrassed when she opened a door to one of the bedrooms and the door knocked a chest of drawers which immediately collapsed! With Derek's generous help and support all these matters were resolved.

My installation was fixed for 24 March 1990 in St John's Cathedral. The service commenced with the traditional three knocks on the closed cathedral doors with my bishop's staff, a custom that was interestingly commented on by many who had never attended an installation before. The *Buenos Aires Herald* rather archaically reported: "The Right Revd David Leake was solemnly installed in his See in St John's Cathedral in this city yesterday by the Primate of the Southern Cone Province, the Most Revd Colin Bazley." My mind reflected on the fact that my father was an honorary canon (emeritus) of the cathedral in Buenos Aires and I like to think that it would have pleased him that his son became bishop of the diocese. He died in 1991.

Diocesan office in Buenos Aires: with Lorna Bateman

Despite this being Buenos Aires, the diocesan office was less pretentious than the one in Salta. It was confined to two rooms with a toilet and small kitchen space on the first floor behind the cathedral, rooms which had been the home of Bishop Every during his long episcopacy (1902-1937). One room was designated as the bishop's office and in the other worked an administrator, his assistant and the bishop's secretary. The cathedral and office are located on a prime site in the centre of the banking district, and in the early days must have been very prominent; today commercial buildings dwarf them. The land value where the building stands must run into millions, but legal and historic restrictions make any alteration or change unlikely. My two immediate predecessors did consider the possibility of selling the plot and being given in exchange the first two floors of the new development, with one floor as a worshipping area incorporating all the cathedral furnishings and panelling, and using the other floor for offices and accommodation for the rector. Another possibility considered was creating and renting out underground car parking facilities. None of these ever got off the drawing board.

The magpie and the policeman

My routine changed greatly from my unstructured and uncertain timetable in the north. Rumour had it that the new bishop did not keep a diary! I was greatly blessed by the willingness of Lorna Bateman de Álvarez, who became my secretary and has remained a great friend to us ever since. She was a committed member of the cathedral congregation and *au fait* with the history and life of the Anglican Church. She has an alert and astute mind and was nicknamed ‘the magpie’ since she was meticulous in keeping detailed information and photocopies of every paper transaction, details which more than once helped us out of difficult situations or served to prove some uncertain decision.

Sadly, a very gifted administrator had to leave a year or two after my appointment, but here again we were greatly blessed with our administrative assistant who assumed greater responsibilities. Oswaldo Balvín, an immigrant from Peru who had served with the police force in complex and dangerous times in inaccessible mountain areas combating the forces of the Shining Path guerrillas, brought a wealth of experience, as well as the mind of a detective, which proved useful many times as we often had to deal with conmen who came feigning to be in need or with some fabricated story of tragedy or disaster. His meticulous and detailed observations also helped in all details of accountancy and he was almost fastidious in his provision of receipts for the most insignificant amount of cash that went across his desk. He was a good public relations figure and became well known to bank managers, solicitors, churchwardens, clergy and others with whom he came to deal, not being fazed by their hierarchy or position, always correct and polite, yet demanding when necessary. Besides these gifts, Oswaldo was as much at home cleaning the cathedral or repairing the drains, and could often be seen up a ladder in pouring rain clearing a gutter.

His police detective experiences stood him in good stead when a man holding a gun was seen in the soup kitchen in the parish hall. I was careful not to raise any alarm and told someone to fetch Oswaldo. He came down and when the man was pointed out he went up to him and said, "I have just noted you on the CCTV screen upstairs holding a revolver." The man was taken completely by surprise and produced a plastic toy revolver that he had picked up from the used clothes trunk! The cathedral certainly had nothing as sophisticated as CCTV —in fact, I was still using a typewriter!—but Oswaldo was always quick to find a way to resolve a problem.

My successor was to face a much more serious situation which could have ended tragically when he and his wife were mugged and their car robbed with the chaplain locked in the boot. In this case Oswaldo's police experience helped in working through a hostage-taking experience, dealing with the hostage-takers on the phone and accompanying the police into a dangerous neighbourhood. All was finally resolved with no ransom paid and the hostages released.

Besides Oswaldo and Lorna, I always felt that the presence of John Woolcock, a regular visitor to the diocesan office, and then after his death Angela Lockwood de Mansilla, kept me on my toes and the accounts straight. As administration is not my forte, I was glad to be surrounded by faithful colleagues and friends.

I became a commuter and would go to the office most days, walking to the station, sometimes changing my route, although probably I was not a likely kidnap victim. The trains on the Tigre-Retiro line were privatised and the service and carriages greatly improved, although issues of safety left much to be desired. There was no provision for exits or means of opening the doors in case of an emergency, and if you did force a door there was a small wooden ladder to climb down which would have landed you on the electric rail. When the air-conditioning worked all was well, but since the windows could not be opened when it did not, which was quite often, you nearly boiled.

The main terminus of Retiro station still bears signs of its British origin, the large metal arches clearly marked 'Made in Liverpool', the buffers in Ipswich, and the obsolete drinking fountains in Kilmarnock.

An enjoyable feature of coming to Buenos Aires was the opportunity to renew contact with many I had been to school with 45 years or so earlier. The monthly lunch for the Old Philomathians I regarded as an opportunity to give the church and the Christian faith a high profile and presence. I was always given a place at the head table and asked to say grace. I must have had some effect. I recall a former boy who would punctuate his public post-prandial storytelling with colourful words and phrases, then guiltily look at me and say, "Sorry, Bishop". I noted that the apologies grew less and less, until one day he was able to tell his stories free of obscenities!

I was invited on various occasions to present the prizes at my old school. This required not just presenting diplomas and books, but greeting each prizewinner with a kiss, even the boys. Kissing between men has become common and acceptable in Argentina as a means of greeting. The subsequent photo-call with the parents meant that prize-giving became quite an extended occasion. One year I woke next morning with aching muscles and realised that my constant bending over to present the prizes had taken its toll!

Explaining work amongst the Indians to Prince Charles on his visit to Buenos Aires

26

A presence far beyond its numbers

ALTHOUGH the Anglican Church in Argentina is not large in numbers or clergy, it does reflect the full breadth of Anglican expression and stands out from most of the other dioceses in the Southern Cone, whose history is linked with more evangelical missionary roots. At the time I left, David George, Archdeacon of the River Plate, kindly wrote in the magazine *Adelante*: "Bishop David brought to the diocese the wisdom and experience of many years as a bishop in the north and this maturity was reflected in his easy acceptance of types of Anglican spirituality that do not exist in the northern diocese. This openness and tolerance have maintained the rich diversity that, in spite of its small size, has always been a mark of the church in Argentina."

Under Bishops Tucker and Cutts, the diocese had moved much more into using Spanish in its worship, services and formal council meetings. Indeed, if the Church did not do this, its days were numbered since the original British community was dwindling and their descendants were more at home in Spanish. Whilst the Cathedral and other churches in Buenos Aires still maintain services in English on Sundays, with good attendance and committed congregations, the main service attended by the younger generation and children is in Spanish. Often coffee is served between services in the parish halls, giving the opportunity for the congregations to meet.

There has been an unofficial moratorium on recruiting clergy from the United Kingdom, obliging the Church to 'grow its own priests locally'. This has been successful, and the ordinations of Agustín Marsal, Brian Williams, Monica Tompkins, the late Roger Hogg, Andrew Lenton, the late Charlie Halperin, Cynthia Dickin, Hernán Dei Castelli, Bertie Hansen, Mario Ágreda, and other more recent ones have proved the policy to be a success. Most surnames reflect British descent, but all these were born in Latin America where their families have their roots. I was the second Argentine-born bishop after my immediate predecessor Richard Cutts.

Clergy training and theological study are provided at ISEDET (*Instituto Superior Evangélico de Teología*), which is recognised as university standard, and the more conservative IBBA (*Instituto Bíblico de Buenos Aires*). Both these houses of ecumenical and interdenominational learning provide broad and adequate theological preparation; complementary teaching on specifically Anglican history and worship are undertaken through diocesan theological extension courses.

We were privileged to see advances both in numbers and commitment. This was particularly true for the work among young people, the Allen Gardiner Memorial Centre in Los Cocos in the Córdoba hills affording an excellent location for the annual camp with up to 90 attending. The enjoyment of these camps was always tinged with a certain anxiety as the children set off and later returned home by chartered double-decker coaches. I always made a point of saying a prayer before the coaches left, and being there with parents and friends when they returned.

Growth was particularly evident in Villa Devoto, where the English-speaking congregation had been reduced to about four. When Agustín Marsal was ordained priest, he was appointed vicar there, and his particular gifts and charismatic experience, together with the support and encouragement of Kenneth and Sheila MacDonald, encouraged the formation of an enthusiastic new congregation of younger members which soon numbered over 100. The worship followed a liturgical pattern with considerable freedom exercised by those leading. The congregation were generous in their giving, making it possible to cover the vicar's stipend from their own offerings.

The Church of the Good Shepherd in Villa Devoto stands in contrast to the cathedral where worship follows traditional Anglican style, this in its way making a valid but contrasting contribution to the mosaic of Anglican life in Buenos Aires. It is difficult to see how much growth can come to the cathedral in its somewhat isolated position, surrounded by city-centre offices, the kind of isolation that has probably affected many city churches where communities have moved out to the suburbs. Its congregation today includes many down-and-outs who attend the soup kitchen in the Parish Hall during the week. It is good to see these people worshipping in a British-style ecclesiastical building with its stained glass windows and war memorials. As a capital city, there is a changing population of expatriate diplomats and business people, as well as English-speaking tourists who see the services announced in the *Buenos Aires Herald.* One trusts that for some it may be a link in a chain on their Christian pilgrimage, and hopefully something they hear or experience may bear fruit on their next stop in Beijing, New Delhi, or wherever.

Following the example of my Episcopal predecessors, I

retained the additional title of Dean of the Cathedral to safeguard any changes or developments with which I might not be in agreement, although the good relationships with the rectors made this unlikely.

Beyond Buenos Aires

Historically, the British community had spread all over the country with the development of the railways and the establishment of farms, so the Anglican Church had a historic commitment to visit these people living thousands of miles from the capital. Those on the farms were referred to as 'people in the camp', using the transliteration of the Spanish word *campo*. I was explaining this to a young British voluntary worker and commented that the diocese used to appoint a Camp Chaplain to visit the *estancias*. The young man looked rather embarrassed and then explained to me that the phrase would have a different connotation in modern-day Britain!

Rachel and I made Easter the time to visit these isolated members of our Church. We enjoyed our visits and from the response we received they seemed to be much looked forward to and appreciated. For me, Argentina had been the northern provinces of Salta, Chaco and Formosa, the hot forest jungle areas of the country with pumas and rattlesnakes. Now our visits took us down to Patagonia with the glaciers, whales and penguins, and as far as the Beagle Channel. It was fascinating to visit the Goodall families who were the descendants of Thomas Bridges, the original Anglican missionary in the area, and of Lucas Bridges, author of *Uttermost Part of the Earth*.

We enjoyed the hospitality of Tom and Natalie Goodall in Harberton, as well as Adrian and Stephanie Goodall in Viamonte, who have remained dear friends. We held services and baptisms at Natalie's home in Tierra del Fuego.

We went to Río Gallegos, where we held the annual service in the chapel of the Roman Catholic bishop and where we would get a good congregation of the descendants of the early sheep farmers. I made a point of taking the service in Spanish since there were younger people who did not speak English. This was met with some resistance, and we were able to come to an amicable solution by having the hymns in English, *Onward Christian Soldiers* being obligatory!

I felt sad that these folk could only have a service once a year, the distance and cost making it difficult to do much more; in European terms, Buenos Aires to Tierra del Fuego is the same distance as London to Istanbul.

Our annual visit to Patagonia took in the 'Welsh Colony'. A glance through the phone book leaves one in no doubt as to the historic Welsh presence: Davies, Jones, Griffiths, Williams, Morgan, and the place names of Trelew, Dolavon, Trevelin and Bryn Gwyn. There is even a 'chapel in the valley': the Anglican Church of St David's in Dolavon was renovated under Bishop Cutts with a generous gift from St David's Cathedral in Wales, and is now zealously cared for by Rebecca Davies, a descendant of one of the early chaplains.

Whilst the establishments of the south are called *estancias* (large farms), those in the area where the Welsh settled are referred to as *chacras* or smallholdings, thus reflecting that these folk were in the main poorer peasants.

Of all the South American colonisers, the Welsh were the most pacific. There is but one recorded incident of confrontation with the Indians, when two Welshmen were killed, and this was because of a genuine misunderstanding. One of the Welshmen managed to escape thanks to his horse 'Malacara' who jumped a narrow gulley, taking his master to safety and earning a worthy epitaph on his tombstone.

When the late Princess Diana of Wales visited Argentina in 1995, it was arranged for her to visit the Welsh colony in Chubut. After a sightseeing tour which included the whales, she was the guest of one of the teahouses. She was taken to the upmarket Ty Caerdydd Té House, owned and managed by Miguel Mirantes, much to the distress of other humbler, yet probably more genuine, smaller houses. After she left, the dregs of her cup were preserved in a bottle and the cup never washed. Together with the tablecloth, these are preserved in a glass case with other memorabilia of her visit.

After her tragic death, I was invited by Miguel Mirantes to arrange a special service in the teahouse. He offered to pay my travel expenses and hotel in Gaimán in order to officiate at the ceremony, which sounded very much like a beatification of Princess Diana and might well turn the teahouse into a kind of sanctuary and tourist attraction. I replied that I would be happy to visit the teahouse, read a portion of Scripture and say a prayer, but would prefer to leave any other pseudo-beatification or blessing to the local Roman Catholic priest. I added that I would not like to be mistaken for his private chaplain and would therefore cover my own travel expenses from the normal regular offerings of the local congregation, so maybe he would be happy to place his contribution in the collection plate on the Sunday. This may all sound rather Jesuitical reasoning but he was happy with the suggestion and I did not feel I had compromised my conscience! All enjoyed a happy ceremony!

A positive step during my time as bishop was to witness and have some share in the development of the work in the city of Mendoza. The Revd Anthony Gregory and his wife Mollie sensed a call to the small remnant of a congregation there, and started services in their own home once a month. Before, the people had only had an intermittent ministry when visited by clergy from Buenos Aires.

In due course services became more frequent and funds were raised locally and from outside to build their own church. A plot of land was bought and a beautiful building erected. This was finished after I left, and appropriately in this wine-producing province was dedicated to the Lord of the Vine-yard! The work continues to progress and is a good example of how to start and develop a new congregation.

Ecumenical activities

Being a capital, cosmopolitan city where over the years many people had immigrated, Buenos Aires has a wide spectrum of churches represented. The predominant one by far is the Roman Catholic, but alongside are the various expressions of Orthodox Churches, the Anglican Church and a wide and broad representation of conservative evangelical denominations, with variant forms of Pentecostal expression.

I was interested to note that the Anglican Church was always identified on its own and was not lumped together with the

Protestant denominations. Although the Anglican Church is small in numbers, it has a long history and the cathedral in Buenos Aires, built in 1831, is reputed to be the first non-Roman Catholic place of worship erected in South America. The decree declaring freedom of worship was promulgated initially for the benefit of the British Anglican community. This place in early history has been maintained, and today the Anglican Church exerts a presence far beyond its numbers. When Bishop Tucker met the Cardinal Archbishop of Buenos Aires, he asked him if there were room and a place for the Anglican Church, thinking in terms of its work in Spanish. The archbishop replied that the spiritual needs of the country were "too big for the Roman Catholic Church, they were too big for the Anglican Church", and finished by saying, "There is room for us all".

A forum called CEICA (*Consejo Ecuménico de Iglesias Cristianas en la Argentina*) had been created for a meeting of the more traditional historic Churches, presided over by a Roman Catholic bishop. I attended the meetings, which were colourful occasions since the Orthodox Greek, Armenian, Antiochean and Russian Churches were always jockeying for hierarchical position and provided interesting dialectic discussion. Maybe it was their inability to sort matters out that led to my invitation to become President of CEICA. This I regarded as an honour since it was the first time the group was to be presided over by someone who was not a Roman Catholic bishop. I also felt my appointment reflected a more ecumenically open attitude by the Roman Catholic Church. Nevertheless, it was no easy task to keep this diverse group of leaders in line!

CEICA was regularly consulted by the press with regard to national religious affairs and sought to give a united Christian voice on issues such as human rights. It was the Methodist Church that had mainly carried the flag in matters of civil rights and they were quite militant in the days of political upheaval, many of their ministers being persecuted and joining the ranks of the 'disappeared' during the period of the Dirty War.

The high point of my time with CEICA was a well planned open-air gathering of all the churches held in the Plaza de Mayo in front of the Metropolitan Cathedral and the historic Cabildo building. This was organised during Holy Week. In my brief dissertation, I quoted the historic cry of early independence day: "*El pueblo quiere saber de qué se trata*". (The people want to know what it's all about.) This was said then with reference to the early murmurings of independence being discussed inside the Cabildo in the 1800s, and I hoped that the people gathered in Plaza de Mayo would be asking the same question of the Christian leaders gathered in the Plaza.

The Cardinal Archbishop Bergoglio and the Patriarch of the Armenian Orthodox Church were the other two speakers; the service included the washing of feet, recalling Jesus' example to His disciples as a symbol of humility. Each time I crossed the Plaza de Mayo after this event and whenever it becomes news as the focus of political upheaval, I like to think that witness was given to Jesus Christ, His love, suffering and resurrection, and pray that from this nerve-centre the Argentine nation may rise to new hopes and values and truly express the Christian faith it professes to believe.

Alongside the traditional liturgical activities, we were involved with two centres caring for babies and small children, allowing their mothers, mostly single parents, to go out and work. This ministry was founded by my predecessor's wife and was the flagship of the Anglican social outreach. But over the years ethos and methods changed, municipal laws and labour regulations became more demanding, making it more and more complicated to keep them going. Fundraising became a headache, and there were months when we did not have enough to pay the carers. On more that one occasion in the diocesan office we had to delay our own salaries to cover the Day Care Centre staff.

27
A visit from Canterbury and other developments

SOON after our arrival in Buenos Aires, Robert Runcie, Archbishop of Canterbury, visited the diocese, accompanied by his wife Rosalind, his secretary, chaplain and the Chaplain of Anglican Affairs. This was a momentous occasion, not only for Anglicans in Argentina, but also at State level since he was designated a visitor of national importance. It was an exciting experience to meet him at Ezeiza Airport and to have a police escort with outriders open up a way through the traffic. Our arrival in Olivos was a rousing event for the neighbourhood.

Once the archiepiscopal entourage had settled in our home, we were allocated a policeman, who stood guard at the door during the day and snoozed in our lounge during the night, his gun on a side table next to him.

An intensive programme had been planned, with internal diocesan visits to churches, ecumenical visits to the religious hierarchy, and a meeting with the President. Only later did we realise what a wonderful opportunity this had given us at the beginning of our ministry in Buenos Aires to have the Archbishop open doors for us, which otherwise would have taken considerable time to achieve.

The meeting in the Casa Rosada, which was attended by leading clergy of the diocese as well as by Government ministers and translators, was amicable. Initially, the conversation related to football and then moved on to more serious subjects,

Archbishop Robert Runcie with Argentine President Carlos Menem

and at the end I suggested that a prayer might be appropriate. President Menem's question was, "Do we sit or do we stand?" I said we would stand and Robert Runcie led us in prayer, which was translated phrase by phrase by the translator.

The visit was obviously seen by the Government as an opportunity to score political points in the matter of improving relations with Britain after the South Atlantic War.

The visit had its lighter moments. One of Robert Runcie's means of relaxation was swimming. We found a small pool not far from our home, significantly called 'Roma'. I was told there would be a free space in the afternoon but that regulations required a qualified lifesaver should be present. I said that my wife Rachel was an excellent swimmer and trained in life saving. This satisfied those responsible, and so in the afternoon we marched round to the pool. The Archbishop followed Rachel and myself, and the armed policeman brought up the rear. Whilst Robert Runcie enjoyed a leisurely swim, Rachel sat by the pool and the policeman at a discreet distance kept guard.

Sharing a joke with Archbishop Michael Ramsey on his visit to Argentina

The Archbishop's visit came to a happy end with more sirens and roaring motorcycle outriders escorting him back to Ezeiza Airport from where he went on to Chile. Once he was back at Lambeth Palace, we received a kind letter thanking us for the hospitality and adding:

"I hope in retrospect the visit lived up to your expectations. I can see what enormous opportunities there are for your new ministry there and what a contrast it must be to your experience in the North. I felt there was great goodwill in ecumenical circles for the Anglican Church and I am sure the diocese has a pivotal place in the life of the Province. I shall watch with keen interest how things develop and hope very much that you will find a real personal satisfaction in all that you set out to do.

"I thought our meeting with President Menem was one of our more productive presidential contacts. I will follow up his suggestion of mediation in regard to Terry Waite [still a hostage at that time], though I believe there may be more complications in his proposal than perhaps he realises."

Both Robert and Rosalind Runcie became good friends and we were later privileged to call upon them in their retirement home when visiting St Albans.

Two sad events

The Revd Ronald Maitland was an American who adopted Argentina as his new home. He was academically well qualified and an able theologian. His particular gift was with students and in his later ministry he became responsible for the San Pablo House for students in Córdoba city, together with being vicar of St Paul's church. Ronald suffered from a serious pulmonary complaint which produced fits of coughing and difficulty in breathing. Towards the end of his life, he lived with us in Olivos before he had to go into the British Hospital. It was a sad day when I was called to the hospital to be told of his death. It was my duty to identify him in the mortuary and to take his funeral. Ronald was buried in the diocesan plot in the British Cemetery in the same burial place as the late Bishop Daniel Ivor Evans.

The Revd Roger Hogg was an exemplary prototype of the ideal Anglo-Argentine Anglican priest. He was of British descent from a family long resident in Argentina; besides Spanish, he spoke fluent English and had a forceful voice and a raucous laugh. Roger had worked as a ranger in the Iguazú National Park. He usually wore his hair long and had a distinctive ginger beard. In the course of a visit with his wife Patricia to Portugal to ascertain the feasibility of initiating an environmental project in the Córdoba hills, he had a haemorrhage and on his return to Argentina was diagnosed with cancer. He faced up to his condition with great fortitude, and on one of my last pastoral visits to him in Córdoba where the students in St. Paul's Hostel (*Casa San Pablo*) were caring for him, I was concerned about the noise in the house. He said he was happy to hear the normal noisy sounds of the boys, and when I asked if anything was concerning him his reply was, "I am concerned for those who are concerned for me".

Roger died aged 39, leaving his wife Patricia and three children. At his funeral I described him as a true *Cura Gaucho* (Gaucho Priest). He would often wear the *bombacho*-style trousers of the *gauchos* and was regularly to be seen drinking his *mate*.

A wise piece of advice that John Woolcock gave me was to establish a small group. He suggested calling it 'BAG' (Bishop's Advisory Group). This sounded threatening at first, but it proved to be a good sounding-board with whom to share matters and ideas. I was not obliged to take their advice, though more often than not I did!

They were quite a mixture—a hard-headed former advertising executive, a leader in one of our charismatic churches, a former colleague from the northern diocese, and an executive sent from the UK to head up his firm's local subsidiary. They were a mixed 'bag', and I purposely chose people different from myself and individuals not afraid to present their opinions forcefully. This group was particularly helpful during the uncertainties and eventual closing of the Day Care Centres.

I was keen to find new ways in which the Church could be committed in its mission and outreach. The traditional methods of evangelism in Latin America were not the style that the Anglican Church would feel comfortable in taking on board; besides which, experience had shown that much that had been done in the name of evangelism had proved shallow and short-lived.

I was aware of the work of A Rocha in Portugal, where Peter and Miranda Harris had developed a successful environmental project of excellence, mainly related to ornithology, and where waste and contaminated marshland had been recovered and become the domain of ornithologists and environmentalists. I felt that we had an excellent opportunity of developing such a project in the Córdoba hills at the Allen Gardiner Centre. The Harrises visited us and encouraged us to move forward. We had ample space and a study was made by Maurice Rumboll, Argentina's leading ornithologist and for many years a lay reader. Forty-six species of birds were identified on land adjacent to the Centre.

I felt that in Roger Hogg we had just the person to develop such a project, but his untimely death meant it did not come to fruition. My hope had been to establish a centre in Argentina where clear Christian environmental principles could be expressed by developing the ongoing work of God's creation and establishing, as in A Rocha, a centre of ornithological excellence, a clear expression of God's purposes in creation, and for Argentina a unique contribution in the area of environmental conservation. The possibility remains that some day something may develop.

Ezeiza Airport for international flights to South America is the end of the line. Most flights return northwards or westwards to Santiago. Our location on the Anglican world map places us at the end of the line; we are geographically isolated. It was, therefore, good news when we were linked through the Partnership in Mission scheme with the dioceses of Niagara (Canada) and Liverpool. This opened up the possibility of exchange visits and some financial support. We were particularly privileged to have a visit from the then Bishop of Liverpool, David Sheppard, who came for the inauguration of the Province of the Southern Cone and my installation as Primate.

This triangular diocesan link-up was not very successful, and after the allotted period it ended. A more positive and successful partnership was to be forged later.

While I was bishop it was possible to establish a link with the Diocese of Sheffield. The bishop at the time, David Lunn, was not a great traveller and reputed not to possess a passport, yet he was nevertheless interested and supportive, and visits were made in both directions. Rachel and I were privileged to be his guests and were sensitively and generously cared for by his Uruguayan housekeeper, whom since his retirement he has married. She was insistent that after lunch we should have a siesta! I was invited to preach in Sheffield Cathedral, a significant and sensitive occasion since much had been made of the sinking of *HMS Sheffield* during the South Atlantic Conflict by the Argentine Air Force. The diocesan link served in some small way to help in the restoring of relationships.

Exchange visits among the young people were particularly positive and exciting, serving to remind us that if we could travel as far as Sheffield we could profitably undertake such visits within the diocese. Some of the young Argentines had never met until they gathered at Ezeiza Airport on their way to Sheffield!

Archdeacon Stephen Lowe, later Bishop of Hulme, was one of the visitors. His traditional British establishment background made for a traumatic time, especially when visiting an *estancia* on the occasion of the traditional *gaucho yerra*. He climbed into the corral with his video camera, but found the branding and castration of the calves and barbecuing of testicles *in situ* just too much!

Although the geographical area of the diocese was large, in terms of numbers it was small. Historically, in ecumenical and State terms, it exerted an influence greater than its numbers would warrant. In terms of the episcopacy, unlike an English diocese, it meant one could know a wide spectrum of church members and in some ways it was more like a large deanery than a diocese. Often during a vacancy it was the bishop who covered for services and for a while I was formally appointed as vicar of the parish of St Saviour's, Belgrano. This gave a special opportunity for 'hands-on ministry' with regular Sunday services, baptisms and weddings, a pastoral opening that I welcomed.

Our days in Buenos Aires proved to be a significant and

happy time. We enjoyed the large house, garden and swimming pool, and our eldest son Andrew with his wife María and the grandchildren from Salta used to look forward to holidays with us. Another highlight was to have them together with our second son Philip, his wife Victoria and the children, and our daughter Judith and her husband Ken Finch. We also had a regular number of diocesan visitors and the occasional volunteer or student living in. It was the venue for many diocesan social events and the annual clergy *asado* (barbecue).

Drawing to a close

The time came to think in terms of future and retirement. We both enjoyed good health and lived in a community that was not retirement-conscious. Tragically many people's retirement and pension plans had been scuppered by economic upheavals and devaluations and many would have to continue to work as long as they could or else maintain part-time employment well past retirement age. We decided I would carry on past my 'sell-by date' and use that time to prepare the diocese and ourselves for the future.

One matter that concerned me was that a key parish like St Saviour's, Belgrano, was without a priest, so our leaving would not only require a new bishop to be elected but also a new incumbent to be designated for Belgrano. After considerable reflection, my thoughts turned to Gregory Venables, the Bishop of Bolivia, and following much prayer and prolonged exchanges with him, we felt it was in line with God's purpose for the diocese that he should be my eventual successor.

This, of course, was not my prerogative to arrange; as I was once reminded, "Only dictators appoint their successors"! But it was an idea that I placed in the hands of the diocese, and when the time came to make proposals a 'package deal' was presented in which Bishop Gregory was invited initially to become the Vicar of St Saviour's, Belgrano, on the understanding that he would also come to the diocese as Coadjutor Bishop—not a known practice in the Anglican Church in the UK, but certainly an arrangement often made in the USA and in the Roman Catholic Church, the Coadjutor Bishop having right of succession on the resignation of the diocesan bishop.

The diocese happily took on board this idea, no other candidates were proposed, and in due course when the Electoral College was convened Bishop Gregory was elected Bishop Coadjutor and came to the diocese as Vicar of Belgrano. This meant that we had two years working together before my retirement, and I was able to leave the diocese in good hands.

Bishop Gregory was already the Presiding Bishop of the Province, an appointment I had held when the Province was first created in 1982, so I was aware of the extra burden of responsibilities this entailed for him. The matters which have concerned the Anglican Church during his primacy have been much more complex than those I had to face.

A couple of months or so before my retirement, I was attending the annual general meeting of the British Hospital. It was a hot evening and some of us were standing outside the Ravenscroft Hall waiting for proceedings to start. The

Ambassador, Sir Robin Christopher, approached me and told me that the Queen wished to award me the honour of becoming a Commander of the British Empire. Would I be happy to accept? I mumbled something about being humbled, and before I could give a considered answer he had moved on to speak to someone else!

I was delighted that the citation was for services to the local and British communities, but I did have some mixed feelings, especially after my heart-searching over taking the oath of allegiance to the Queen before my consecration. I was happy to think that work undertaken in the name of Christ and His Church was recognised. At an ecumenical meeting in Buenos

At Buckingham Palace with Rachel, Philip and Judith

Aires, Bishop Venables humorously announced that he did not think there was much empire left, but it now had a good commander!

I was allowed three guests at the investiture, so Rachel, Philip and Judith accompanied me. We had planned to get a taxi to Buckingham Palace, but Graeme Le Saux, England international footballer and brother-in-law to our son Andrew and his wife María, kindly provided a chauffeur-driven saloon, so we arrived in style. It was a happy and memorable day, all so far removed from my childhood under the shady algarrobo trees of Sombrero Negro!

Honoured by the Queen

28
Privileged to go on serving

OUR last few months in Buenos Aires were full with sorting out papers and handing things over to Bishop Gregory. Looking back on my early lifetime and almost 40 years' ministry together with Rachel, I feel very privileged to have been close witnesses of big changes amongst the Indians, the completion of the whole Bible in Wichi and the New Testament in Toba, the formal recognition and documentation of the Indians as full Argentine citizens, the openings for the new generation to secondary education, the ordination of many to ministry in the Church and the consecration of the first Indian bishop. To see the younger generation adapt with great rapidity to the digital age when their grandparents had no written language is a remarkable privilege.

Rachel with Toba girls during a recent visit

New generation of Toba children

Our time in Buenos Aires too was a great experience, being part of a Church adapting to new realities. The upsurge and increase in younger members to the Church, the proactive work and activities organised by the Marriage Encounter group and the increase in number of Argentine-born ministers, thus breaking the dependence on expatriate clergy.

Rachel and I decided we would carry on until was I was 67; this gave us a couple of years over normal retirement age in our home in Olivos. Time was spent planning our retirement and where it should be; we would have been happy to retire in Argentina, but it could be unfair on our successors, both in the northern diocese as well as in Buenos Aires. We had been relatively close to Andrew and María and the family, and we felt it would be nice to have some time close to Philip, Victoria and the children, and Judith and her husband Ken in the UK. The factor that tipped the balance was that we had a home there, having inherited the family cottage in Norfolk where my parents and their parents before them had lived.

Many people generously expressed their appreciation of our time in the diocese. We had been blessed in seeing encouraging developments, mainly among the young people and local candidates for ordination, which are good omens for the continuing and strengthening of the work. We had had to face many difficult decisions and severe financial restrictions. Love was tangibly expressed in the presentation to us of innumerable silver engraved trays and signed parchments which today decorate our cottage and remind us of our happy years in Buenos Aires, together with mementos and artefacts from the Indians which recall a most significant part of our lives and those of our family.

Our packing and removal, though expensive, was made easy by a professional firm of excellence who came to the house and pre-packed delicate items and placed them in pre-moulded cardboard boxes. Everything gradually disappeared into the neat boxes which were then loaded into a container. Our bedroom furniture, made in Misión Chaqueña of algarrobo wood, was also packed. It was a great relief when all was loaded on a truck in Olivos and it started its long journey from Buenos Aires to East Runton.

We were overwhelmed by the numerous expressions of

My father Alfred with Bishop Mario on a visit to Cromer

gratitude and farewells arranged by many groups, the climax being the memorable service held in the cathedral with the cover of the liturgy entitled *Acción de Gracias por el ministerio del Obispo David Leake y Rachel Leake en la Diócesis de Argentina* (Service of Thanksgiving for the ministry of Bishop David Leake and Rachel Leake in the Diocese of Argentina). I looked back to the 1940s when, as a schoolboy, I used to attend the Empire Day service in the cathedral, and now I was being bade farewell as the bishop. I remembered how as we used to fly over Buenos Aires Rachel regularly prayed with gratitude that we did not have to live there, and now we were leaving after 12 happy years of ministry.

Multum en parvo

We were pleased to set up home in our family cottage by the sea in Norfolk. Our son Philip had been our link person with a local builder, Tim McCrohon, who had worked excellently and turned a rather damp and cold cottage into a cosy home. The arrival of our belongings from Argentina added to the furniture and items and papers left by my parents, and made us realise how small the cottage was. A few bumps on my forehead forcibly reminded me how low the doors were!

We had to be ruthless in sending items to auctions and the tip, and have become regular contributors to charity shops. I have had to learn not to live in the past, and to limit myself to what is of historical value with regard to papers and books. It is so true that if you streamline and have things in order, it's good for the soul.

Ongoing ministry

Bishop Graham James was now Bishop of Norwich. I first met him when as chaplain to the Archbishop of Canterbury he came to stay with us in Buenos Aires. He kindly invited me to become an Honorary Assistant Bishop in the diocese, and I was also invited to assist in the benefices of Runton and Cromer, all of which gives me opportunity still to be of service. None of these commitments is too onerous, and I have had ample time to continue a close involvement with the work of translating the New Testament into the Toba language, a task my father started just over 70 years ago. The translation project was undertaken by Michael Browne and three Toba Indians, and the completed New Testament was launched and

With Michael Browne and Toba translators

dedicated in 2010. With the use of computer software and various return visits to Northern Argentina, I was able to collaborate with Michael and the team to help make this momentous event possible.

Pastor Quichi receives the first Toba New Testament

On our return visits to Argentina, we have been able to enjoy time with Andrew, María and the grandchildren. Andrew works among the same Indian peoples as did we and my parents before us in the Argentine Chaco; his task is to support and empower them with logistical information and mapping to help with their land claims. Philip and Victoria work for the NHS in England as psychiatric nurse and occupational therapist respectively, while Judith and Ken now live and work in Kiwoko hospital in Uganda. It is a great satisfaction to know that all our children are serving God and people in different ways.

A year or so after retirement in the village of East Runton, I was invited to preach on St Andrew's Day. The village church is dedicated to that saint and the building is the room of the ancient village school, the very classroom where my father had been taught as a boy and where in retirement he had served as honorary assistant curate.

Developments in the Indian Church, and the increased numbers of gifted, qualified and dedicated missionaries, made me reflect on the inspiring spirit of St Andrew. Little is said of him in the Bible except that he was a good net-worker. On being called by Jesus, he called his brother Simon Peter, whose commitment to the Gospel and the Church was second to none. Had he not been invited by Andrew, we might not have heard anything further of him.

Andrew was also the person who noted the potential in small things. He brought the boy with the five loaves and two fishes, which Jesus took to feed 5,000. At the ordination services where my father had assisted and translated for the

Bishop, I was often reminded that, like Andrew who responded to God's call and left his father with the boat by the Sea of Galilee, so my father left his father in the boat by the shore in East Runton. With his own limited qualifications in God's hands, he was able to achieve great things in introducing many Indians to Jesus Christ and see a truly strong Church come into being from basic and unpromising beginnings. It is not without significance, too, that the first church and mission on the River Pilcomayo initiated by my father in 1927 is dedicated to St Andrew.

Finale or *Bueno time*

Bueno time was a phrase coined by my mother which she used when she felt a conversation or meeting should be closed.

I have been privileged to live a full life. My natural gifts of Indian languages, Spanish and English and my dual nationality as an Argentine born of British parents have given me special opportunities in ministry, and circumstances have enabled me to use these gifts. I always feel I should have done so much more, and trust God to forgive my failures and lost opportunities.

What I can say is that these natural circumstantial gifts, coupled with God's calling to the Christian ministry, have provided a most exciting and satisfying life, and if I had life over again there is little I would change, except the mistakes I have made.

A recent photograph of the family

Appendix 1

Captain Allen Gardiner to the Chiefs of the Toba Nation
Banner Cove, Tierra del Fuego 1851

THIS letter comes to you with greeting.

Our country, which is called Great Britain, lies far, very far from yours; a great sea of three moons divides us. We cannot come to you to speak face to face, but we send one of our people to tell you what is in our hearts. Our God, whom we serve has made us great and happy, and we desire to see all nations as great and happy as we are. This God, who has done such great things for us, is the only true God. He made the Heavens and the earth, and the sea, and all things in them, and He has given us a Book in which we are taught all that He would have us do, and where our spirits will go where we die, for the spirit that is in us lives for ever.

We have sent this Book to many other nations, and all who have received it have been made happy, and wished that they had known it sooner. Why should the Toba nations be the last to receive this Book? It grieves us to think that you are still ignorant of it; we therefore now offer it to you as the best present we can send you. The Tobas are a brave people, and we doubt not they will prove themselves as wise as they are brave by accepting this proof of our goodwill and friendship towards them. We pray you not to think lightly of the offer which we now make, for when once you have heard the words of that precious Book, you will value it as we do. We would not part with it for all the riches of the world.

We were once without this Book, as you are now, and then all things went ill with us, but since we have known the good and comfortable words which it contains we have been made happy; and, besides this, we are bound to send it to you, for it is commanded in that Book, that those who have it should send it out to all the nations of the world, until they are all provided with it.

This then, O Chiefs, is our message to you. Let two of our people visit you, let them dwell with you securely until they have learned to speak to you in your own language. They will then be able to read the good words of God's Book in your ears and make you glad. They will come cheerfully, without fear, for why should they be afraid? We do not think so ill of the brave Toba nations as to suppose that they will do any harm to our messengers who come with words of peace. No, we feel assured that they will take care of them. One of them will be a medical man, well informed in all that is necessary, in order to cure or alleviate all kinds of diseases.

Every six moons we will send some little present to your great captain, in order that you may not forget your distant friends, as they never can p-ass to your country.

Again we say to you, chiefs, and to all the Toba nation, our hearts are towards you. We are your friends although you know it not; and, though we cannot speak together, we can listen to the words of the same Book, which tell us to love all men, to call them our brethren, and to do good to them as we have opportunity. We will continue to pray to our God to bless you, to incline your hearts to receive His Word, and that you may continue to live in peace on the land of your fathers, no man disturbing you in your possessions.

Farewell, captains, and all the Toba nations. May you be forever happy.

YOUR FOREIGN FRIENDS

Appendix 2

Sermon preached in Westminster Abbey on the occasion of renewal of diplomatic relations between Argentina and Great Britain

"WHEN my phone rang early one morning a few weeks ago and I received an invitation to preach at this service, I immediately consulted the Argentine ministry responsible for Religious Affairs and spoke to Dr Angel Centeno and also to the British *chargé d'affaires*, Mr Alan Hunt; they both wholeheartedly encouraged me to accept the invitation.

"My role today, however, is not to play the amateur diplomat; it is, I believe, to try to bring to the whole sad affair of the South Atlantic war and its aftermath a prophetic message from God.

"Those of us Argentines of British descent who had sons of military age at the time of the conflict, one with British nationality and the other with Argentine nationality, lived the anguish of contradictions. I know of one family who had one serving in the Royal Navy and the other doing his national service in the Argentine Army ….. thankfully they did not meet in conflict.

"Today we come to thank God for bringing us so far along the road of reconciliation. We have moved a long way in a short time, thanks to the wise and sensitive conversations and decisions of our diplomats, and the quiet groundwork being done by the South Atlantic Council, the Argentine-British

Society and other groups and individuals.

"We must not be satisfied with the *status quo ante bellum*; if so, we will be giving credence to the cynics who see recent rapprochements as merely terms for establishing a situation favourable to trade and commerce. But even less should we be satisfied with it because it is less than I believe God demands of us.

"Last Sunday I was preaching in one of my churches in the suburbs of Buenos Aires. My Easter message made reference to the costliness of true reconciliation …. through His suffering upon the Cross … Christ reconciled us to Himself and gave us the ministry of reconciliation.

"One's heart still bleeds when one thinks of the war, its tragedy and senselessness so clearly expressed by Argentina's man of letters, Jorge Luis Borges, who was still alive at the time of the conflict and wrote this poem translated into English by Rodolfo Terragno:

'Juan López and John Ward'

'It was their fate to live in a strange time,
the planet had been carved into different countries each one
provided with loyalties
with loved memories
With a past which doubtless had been heroic
With ancient and recent traditions
With rights
With grievances
With its own mythology

With forebears in bronze
With anniversaries
With demagogues and symbols
Such an arbitrary division was favourable to war.
López had been born in the city next to the motionless river
Ward in the outskirts of the city through which Father Brown had walked
He had studied Spanish so as to read Quixote.
The other professed a love for Conrad, revealed to him in a class in Viamonte Street.
They might have been friends, but they saw each other just once.
Face to face in Islands too well known, and each one was Cain, and each one Abel.
They buried them together.
Snow and corruption know them.
The story they tell happened in a time we cannot understand.'

"Sadly, history proves that lessons are not learnt and tragedies are repeated. One of Britain's leading literary figures, Dr Samuel Johnson, in 1771 wrote an essay on the Falklands crisis of his time in which he urged Britain not to use force to resolve rights to all the islands. He states, 'If one party resolves to demand what the other resolves to refuse, the dispute can be determined only by arbitration; and between powers that have no common superior there is no other arbitrator than the sword.'

"Argentina and Britain are both countries that would recognise Christian roots, and may I suggest that it is only in the measure in which we seek together to invoke and implement Christian principles and values into international discussions and decisions that we will reach a true and lasting peace.

"We need to humble ourselves before Almighty God. The English mind and the Latin heart need to meet. We need to understand why we each think and act as we do. We need to appreciate the completely different concepts between the immutability of codified Roman law, upon which the Argentine legal system is based, and the concept of law as something that evolves, with acts of precedents and accumulating jurisprudence, as in the British legal system.

"We thank God today for where we have got to in our relations. May I urge you to pray for our leaders whose responsibility is to continue developing deeper relationships, trust and understanding, so that we may reach a level of reconciliation which satisfies God's standard of justice.

"This could well call us to move forward to find completely new ways of deciding the future of the islands. The Gospel calls us not to claim our rights, but to give them up.

"St Paul describes our Lord Jesus Christ as one who though He was Himself God did not claim equality with God. He did not claim His rights as God. He forewent His rights in order to redeem a fallen creation. As those to whom He has entrusted the ministry of reconciliation, how are we to redeem the tragic situation of the Malvinas/Falklands? How do we make them now into a symbol of peace and lasting reconciliation?

"The Psalmist reminds us (24.1): *'The earth is the Lord's and everything in it....'*

"God is Sovereign—not any particular country or group of people at some particular point in history. Maybe we could best express His Sovereignty by together transforming the islands in question into some kind of reserve for the benefit of all mankind, making it a base and centre for the conservation of the whole of Antarctica, and by so doing transform the Malvinas/Falklands from a symbol of friction and war into a symbol of love and peace.

"Let us place this whole question into a Divine context and apply prayerfully to it the words of Isaiah (2.4): *'He shall judge among the nations and shall decide for many people, and they shall beat their swords into ploughshares and their spears into pruning hooks; nation shall not lift up sword against nation, neither shall they learn war any more'.*

"May it so be, for only when we include God as revealed in Jesus and His Divine concepts of peace and justice in our deliberations and actions will we have grounds for a lasting thanksgiving for reconciliation."

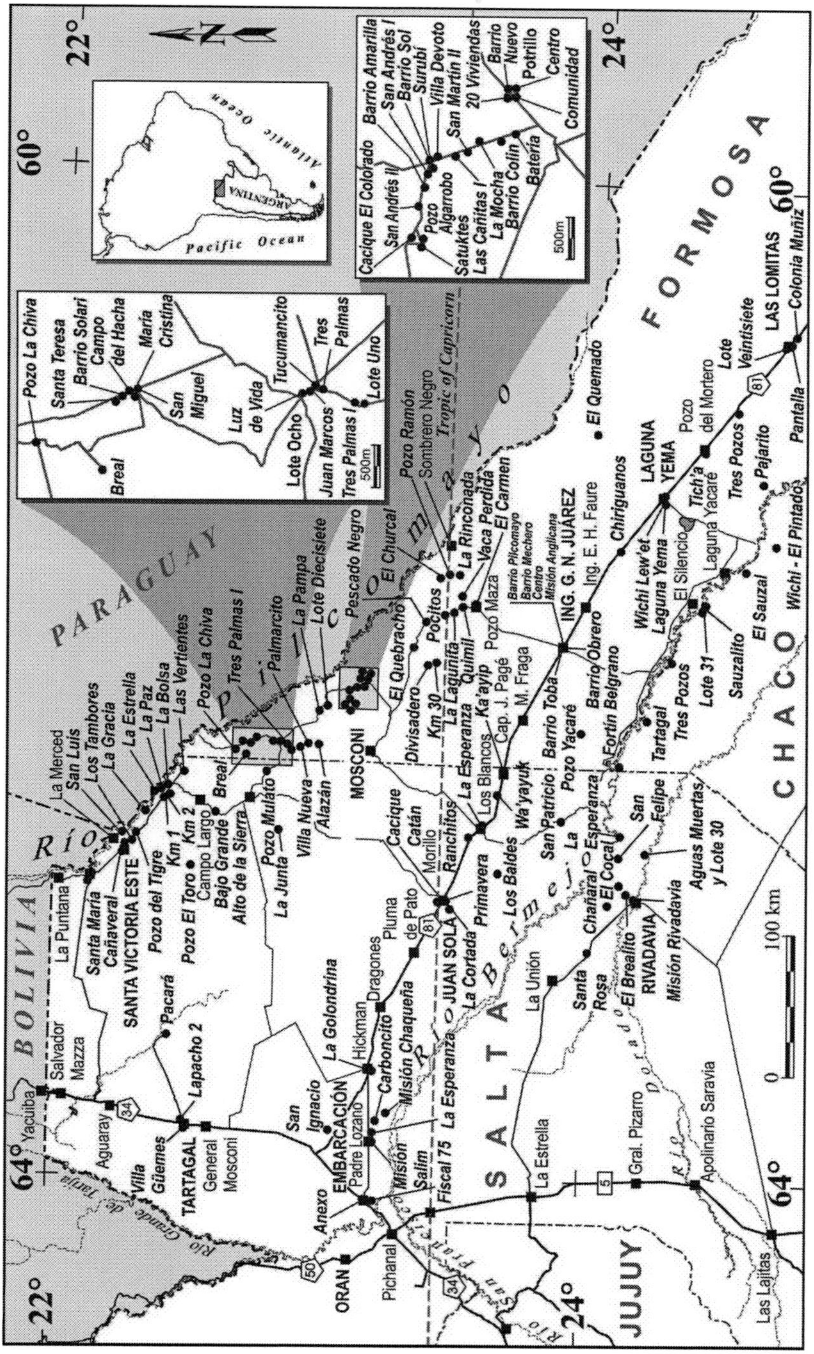

Indigenous communities and Anglican congregations (shown in italics)
Source: Adapted from *Diócesis Anglicana del Norte Argentino*, 2011
Map by Enrique O. López

Glossary

asado	barbecue
aguante	endurance
algarrobo	South American carob tree
alpargatas	shoes made from canvas with rope soles
boliche	small general store
bombacha	baggy trousers
botica	first aid centre, dispensary
bueno	well; okay
CACTM	Central Advisory Council for the Training of the Ministry
camión	lorry
campo	countryside
carona	leather padding on which saddle rests
Chaco	Hunting land. Area inhabited by Indians in Northern Argentina
Chacra	smallholding
chagas	tropical parasitic disease (American *trypanosomiasis*)
chañar	tree with small yellowish flowers and edible berries *(Geoffroea decorticans)*
chaqueño	cowboy settler in the Chaco
charqui	meat cut in strips and dried in the sun
coca y bic	coca and soda bicarbonate
cola	queue
coleto	rawhide leather protective jacket
CRB	Criminal Records Bureau
cura gaucho	gaucho priest
Día del Telefonista	Day of the Telephone Operator
estancia	large cattle establishment

GLOSSARY

gaucho Argentine cowboy
gringo Spanish slang to denote westerners
guardamonte rawhide leather to protect from thorns
häp (wichi) very common word which refers to something just mentioned
hinchar (Argentine slang) being a nuisance
incommunicado isolated prisoner
indígena Indian
Iniciativa Cristiana Christian Initiative
kachagaik (Toba) thief
¡Libertad! Liberty!
Libreta de Enrolamiento Identity Document
mañana tomorrow
mate drink made from green tea; also gourd from which it is drunk
NGO Non Government Organisation
"Pepe thaye Ema" (*wichi) "Pepe and Ema"*—title of a first reader
pajarera large cage enclosure for prisoners
palo santo wood used for engraving *(bulnesia sarmientoi)*
patear to kick
poncho cape with slit for head
problema problem
quebracho evergreen hard tree (axebreaker)
Raquel Rachel
Si...si Yes…yes
sulky light two-wheeler drawn by horse/mule
Teléfono del Obispado telephone at the bishop's residence
Toba ethnic group

turco	Turk, but commonly denoting all of Arab descent
vinchuca	insect *(Reduviidae),* carrier of *chagas* disease
yerba	green tea *(ilex paraguariensis)*
yerra	cattle/horse branding
yica	Indian string bag

Index